W9-CLJ-133

The Real Woman
in the Religious Life

The Real Woman
in the Religious Life

by John J. Evoy, S.J.
and Van F. Christoph, S.J.

SHEED AND WARD : NEW YORK

ACKNOWLEDGMENTS Scripture translations in this book are from *The Holy Bible,* Confraternity Edition. Copyright 1962 The Confraternity of Christian Doctrine.

Foreword

In the summer of 1965 the authors gave a series of twenty-four conferences for meditations to a group of women religious. Most of the conferences were given by both authors, who simultaneously occupied the platform and took turns speaking. An occasional conference, however, as indicated in the text, was given by only one of them.

Over the past two years the authors have reworked the conferences for publication. Since this reworking was done within the framework of the original format, it was decided to retain that format in the published version.

Contents

The Real Woman
in the Religious Life

1 *The Real Woman*

Fr. Evoy: It is related of St. Theresa of Avila that she was once critically short of funds when she desired to build a new convent. "With only a few coins," someone asked her, "what could you possibly hope to do?" She answered immediately, "With only a few coins, Theresa can hope to do very little; with only a few coins and Christ, Theresa can hope to do a great deal." In these words she was referring to the strikingly beautiful truth that when, out of love, a good woman places her hand in that of Christ, there is no limit to her power.

When you took your religious vows, you placed your hand in Christ's. It is of the utmost importance that you recognize there is more than one way in which one's hand can be placed in another person's. A small frightened child can hold the hand of an adult. She does so mainly to get security. It is not a giving of herself to the other person that is signified by the hand holding, but rather it is a gesture through which the child's need is fulfilled.

An adult can, from love, place her hand in that of another adult. When she does so, it should be a giving action, not a getting one. The real woman, who through her religious vows and the living of them places her hand firmly and tenderly in that of Christ, is by that action giving herself to him. When this is what is taking place, there is no limit to what she can do for him and to what he can accomplish for his kingdom through her.

But, unfortunately, besides real women, there are also what might be termed little old girls, who through their religious vows cling to Christ's hand. Their relationship to Christ tends to resemble a security blanket. Their contact with him calls to mind the picture of a frightened child clinging frantically to a strong person. Although he may employ them in his divine providence, with and through such as these who are not real women Christ does not accomplish great things for the salvation of men.

This fact we must face squarely. It is simply not correct to think that anyone who pronounces religious vows and then becomes an observant religious is, by that reason, a highly effective instrument in the work of the kingdom of Christ. A female does not automatically become a real woman by the act of pronouncing vows nor by being religiously observant. Unless such a person works diligently and continuously at becoming a real woman, she will remain a female in religious life. Since a sister's vocation, which is to live her life, out of love, under religious vows for the spreading of Christ's kingdom, will be realized only to the extent that she is a real woman, great efforts should be made by religious communities to help her to become such.

Recently a prominent visitor from outside this country stated that, in his judgment, the women religious of America constitute the greatest single factor for the growth and welfare of the Church in the United States. This is and will probably be true only to the extent that these women religious are real women.

What is the portrait of the real woman that every sister should strive to become? Perhaps men are particularly aware of the inexpressible greatness of a real woman. At any rate, it is unmistakable to a man when he encounters such a woman. At the same time he realizes that since her admirable qualities defy exact expression, any adequate presentation of what is seen in her is impossible.

Nevertheless, in the hope that no matter how halting the language you will know immediately what is being communicated, here is an endeavor at her partial portrait: The real woman is a deeply honest person. Encountering basic dishonesty in another leaves her feeling almost sick because of what the dishonesty is doing to the person using it and especially to others. While she may at times be far from certain that her judgment is correct, she nonetheless endeavors to follow what seems right to her and, at the same time, tries to remain open to correction.

She is real. At times she too has wondered how acceptable to others her personality is. She refuses, however, to pretend to act like someone else or play a role in order to win acceptance. Neither does she use speech dishonestly in order to court acceptance and favor. She has, however, a basic acceptance of herself. She does not dislike herself. While she may, at a particular time, be ashamed of something she has done, she is never ashamed of herself as a person. Her consistency flows from her own characteristic way of thinking and reacting. While her feelings may on occasion be exceedingly strong, her habitual pattern is to refuse to be enslaved by those feelings. Hence, regardless of how she feels, she can be depended on to somehow manage to act the way she judges she should, rather than according to the way she feels.

She is feminine to the fingertips, with all the wonderful warmth and concern implicit in this expression. And she is strong as only a woman ought to be strong. There is nothing soft, flabby, or vacillating about her view of the things that matter greatly to her. Without hesitation she senses when something is wrong or suspect, whether or not she is able immediately to explain why. She is certain of what values she lives by and she can be counted on to stand by them. She says openly what she thinks about something, when such openness is in her judgment called for.

She is capable of loving warmly without having in the least to be concerned about slipping into any inappropriate sentimental expressions. She really cares about other people, as people, regardless of every other consideration. In her love there is a certain singlemindedness. So calmly preoccupied is she with the welfare of those she loves that, without the slightest trace of the "self-sacrificing martyr," she gladly spends herself for others. Consequently she has relatively little time to be concerned about herself. Her love for others spontaneously flows forth in fitting ministrations to them. In her love she is constant, knowing nothing of the pattern of blowing hot and cold, of being unsure. There is not even a shadow of fickleness in her love. The constancy of her love is one of the things in this world that can be depended on.

With the passing of time, she becomes a good judge of the character of others. Sham and the nongenuine cannot hide from her penetrating gaze. But she does not attack or criticize others in their absence. Character assassination not only is foreign to her, but so aware is she of its lethal nature that even to witness it leaves her nauseous. On the other hand, she does not hesitate, no matter how afraid or uncomfortable she is in so doing, to tell others what she thinks she ought to tell them, pointing out their behavior which is hurtful to others and so needs to be mentioned for the good of all concerned. She is patient, kind, or completely forgiving where one of these is the appropriate expression of her love for another. Finally, she is a happy person. Her presence is warmly reassuring, for she radiates love and goodness as only a real woman can.

Such is the incomplete portrait of the real woman. Our Lady, of course, is the foremost example of the real woman. The sister who, in large part, measures up to this criterion of what she could and should be is a delight to God and man. She is, moreover, one with and through whom our Lord can accomplish so much for the building up of his Mystical Body.

2 *Sin*

Fr. Christoph: The *for-God-ness* about which we sometimes speak is characteristic of everything that is. As we all know, things less than man are to get to God through man in the sense that they are to aid man in his journey back to God. Man is to go directly to God. But we are not always conscious of our *for-God-ness*. Too often we act as if we were made for ourselves. When we seek ourselves rather than God, we introduce disorder into our lives. Our destination is supposed to be God-ward. Often when we seek other creatures, we seek them for our own purposes in disregard of God's purposes. This use of creatures in a way that is deliberately opposed to God's will is called sin. The unfortunate reality is that we all have some tendency toward inordinate self-seeking. And we all are sinners. This should not be too surprising to us as religious since even we remain human beings, endowed with human drives and tendencies. We must all admit with embarrassment that we have to some extent failed to measure up to the full implications of our vocation. We can slip into faults, serious defects, and even deliberate sins. We must reflect upon our behavior in an effort to discover the sources of our personal failures.

Even if we have no serious sins about which to be concerned we do have our defects, and our desire of growing to full personal spiritual stature in the service of Christ should make us concerned about them. Moreover, with the current emphasis on the Mystical Body and the relationship of each individual to it, the consequence of everyone's behavior takes on new spiritual dimensions. If that behavior is notably below what it should be, it does not remain a private matter. St. Paul reminds us that we are all "members, one of the other." Newspapers, radio, and the TV daily report violence and crime which affect the body of mankind not only in the secular but also in the spiritual order. We should be deeply concerned about the whole human community, especially those of the household of the faith who by their actions have brought tragedy to the Whole Christ. So our thoughts are now going to be concerned with the nature and the consequences of sin.

Fr. Evoy: Sin is very difficult for us to comprehend because it is not a thing. Sin is the absence of a thing. Moreover, it is the absence of something which ought to be there. We have no tangible grasp of such an absence. Let me clarify this. Suppose, for instance, someone were brought into the emergency room with an arm torn out at the shoulder. We would see the gaping socket left. This is a privation, which means an absence of something which should be there. But this kind of privation we can understand because we actually see the gap where something should be.

In sin, however, we have no such tangible evidence of what is wanting. There is nothing about the privation which sin is that can be perceived by our senses. Besides, to add further to our difficulty in appreciating the reality of sin, we must recall that sin is rooted in the mystery of evil and is ultimately resolvable only in the mystery of Christ. Despite the difficulty of penetrating with our unaided intellects to the core of sin, we do recognize that sin is the greatest evil in the world.

In attempting to grasp why sin is an evil, it might be helpful to reflect that sin is always hurtful to oneself or to others. No matter how private a sin is, it always damages one God loves.

When I look at this fact in terms of the Mystical Body, which Father Christoph was just mentioning, I see still another aspect of the hurtfulness of sin. I simply cannot sin and then wall off this sin so that it affects me exclusively. I cannot confine its hurtful effects solely to my person. In fact, if I employ the closest parallel to the Mystical Body available, that of man's physical body, this point becomes even more clear. When, for example, a person receives a bullet wound in a vital area of the body, the damage is not confined to the one member receiving the wound. His whole body in all of its members is radically damaged even though it is only this one member which has directly received the wound.

So too, in the Mystical Body of Christ, every serious wound to any one member is hurtful to the Whole Christ. And since the individual members share in the vitality of the Whole Body, serious damage to any one member indirectly has a hurtful effect on each of the others. This includes not only those members with whom I live here and now but also others in faraway places. It includes even those who have lived before me and those who will live after me. In some real way I am united with each of them, and so this wound of my sin is such that they are also damaged by it. No matter how difficult for me to grasp, this is literally true.

There is another consideration which I should like to touch upon in this context. It is the Fatherhood of God. I am not mine; you are not yours. In terms of true ownership, I belong completely to God. You belong completely to God. Your role here is one of stewardship. It is one of taking care of, of employing properly that which God has entrusted to you. Whom has he entrusted to you? To you he has entrusted not only you but also everyone whom you know. Starting right in your community, each one of you has been entrusted by God with the becoming care of your sister. You *are* your "sister's keeper." God has put her in your care. This trust is at once a precious gift and a tremendous responsibility.

Since sin is always a privation, you can sin against your sister just by not really caring about her. Your sin with regard to her and others under your charge is that of not really *being* to them. Each of them needs you—needs your love, your concern, your interest, your attention, your friendship, perhaps even your for-giveness. Your sin can consist in solely withholding yourself from these persons in terms of your not really *being* to them. Sin does not necessarily mean the using of another person. Using a per-son is but one way of sinning against another. You can sin more easily by failing to love that person, failing to be your "sister's keeper."

Fr. Christoph: There is something positive, too, in the exercise of this stewardship about which Father Evoy was speaking. We have pressing responsibilities toward others that could be frightening. We should not be too apprehensive, but we should face the consequences of responsibility. Your talents, your physical health, your work—these are responsibilities, the carrying out of which is an essential part of your commitment. To the extent that it is willful, bad stewardship implies a lack of appreciation of the responsibilities that are yours. Hence shame should be aroused in you for your shortcomings in fulfilling your obligations to yourself, to other people, especially to your confreres in religious life.

There is a tremendous gift of God in the capacity to sin or not to sin. This is your freedom. You do not have to sin. It is the abuse of this gift—freedom—that makes sin so totally un-becoming in the eyes of God. It should make you disgusted with yourself. If you *had* to act in this manner, you would never be responsible, culpable, or even ashamed. Up to a point you sin because you want to, because you deliberately choose to, while knowing that this is not what you should be doing. This is the abuse of one of the most wonderful gifts that God has given you, that of free will.

Another humiliating reflection is that so often in religious life your sins have for their object other members of the religious community. For, after all, many of the sins you commit are violations of fraternal charity. If you look upon your fellow religious as other Christs, then you see the meanness, the smallness, the terribleness of your behavior in terms of abusing Christ in your religious sisters. You do not think enough, it seems to me, of the fact that you are to be Christ to your neighbor and you are to see your neighbor as Christ. I used to say, "See Christ in my neighbor," but I think it is more correct to say, "See my neighbor as Christ." When you become aware of that truth—and you should make yourselves aware of it—your behavior will be either more meritorious or more deserving of condemnation, because you will be acting with a comprehension of the critical realities of stewardship, of freedom, of Christ in yourself—of yourself as Christ, and of your neighbor as Christ.

Fr. Evoy: I should like to add a few words to Father Christoph's remark that whereas he used to say he saw Christ *in* his neighbor, he now says that he sees his neighbor *as* Christ. While we do not disregard the element of mystery in seeing our neighbor *as* Christ, we are nevertheless not wholly without understanding in this matter.

Does the act of loving your sister in the community as Christ wishes mean that you turn your eyes away from all that is unlovely in her and, thus undistracted by what is personally unacceptable in her, strive to see only Christ *in* her? By no means. It is by loving the real her with a love that takes the acceptable and encourages her to change the unacceptable in herself that you are loving Christ. That is the way Christ loves her and wants you to love her.

In our Lord's description of the Last Judgment, did he say, "Since you really intended to do it for me when you did it to these other people, I'll overlook the fact that you were doing it to them and give you credit for doing it to me"? Quite the contrary. He said, "Whatsoever you did to even the least of these my little ones, you did to me." There is nothing in these words about closing your eyes to the individual person and imagining that beneath "this all too, too human flesh" you see him. He simply says that whatever you did to them you did to him.

But should this be such a surprising way to view the matter? After all, if you were to do something to one of my bodily members, say that you were to bandage my hand, would you not be doing it to me and would not this still be true even if my hand were soiled or disfigured? What our Lord, then, is saying is that when you do something to this person precisely as she *is* with all her idiosyncrasies, you are doing it to him.

Sisters, I think that in one sense you have an advantage over religious men. To the point that you are real women, the motherly in you can respond to the weak, the needy, the helpless. All about you, even among your own sisters, you see those who in some real sense are weak, in need, and powerless to grow without your real care. Could not these needs of your own sisters and of others call forth the motherly in you when and if you let them?

God has told you to love others. When he said, "Love one another," he was telling you that your love was to include men, women, boys, and girls. And he said, "Love them as I have loved you." This he stated as a new commandment. And while he has not furnished you with a blueprint showing you how to love others, he did tell you to love them "as I have loved you." How does he love you? Is he carried away with sentimentality? By no means. His love for you is a warm, personal, considerate, and therefore controlled love. We might note in passing that our Lord here gives us the hallmark of every genuine love—that it considers the good of the one *loved* rather than the need of the one *loving*.

Christ's love for each person is genuine. At the grave of Lazarus the personal nature of Christ's love was so manifest that those present said openly, "See how he loved him."

Never for a moment should you forget that our Lord's love for you is the real love of the God-man for this person who is *you*. His love is no impersonal disposition of good will and kindness toward humanity. He gave himself for each of you. That is what St. Paul is referring to when he says, "He suffered for me." That is real love, love so great that he surrendered to death for you. And that love was and is intensely personal. Love always is. Moreover, he wants you to love him and to love others as he has loved you. Refusing to love is wrong. Deliberately failing to love is sinful, and as Father Christoph indicated earlier, sin is always a lack of charity.

Fr. Christoph: We can go one step farther and qualify our love. Our love for our neighbor must be the kind of love that Christ has for us. And we have been reminded that Christ loves us just as we are. His love is a forgiving love. *He* loves us despite our defects, our shortcomings, and our failures to live up to the singular commitment that is ours as human beings, as Christians, and as religious.

In salvation history we find examples of the justice of God meted out to sinners in which, from our point of view, this merciful, forgiving aspect is not evidenced to the same extent that we discover it in God's attitude towards us.

Go back to the first example of the creature's refusal to acknowledge God as the source and fulfillment of his existence. We do not see the evidence of God's forgiving love toward the angels who in a chorus under Lucifer declared they would not serve. If we analyze the nature of God, we recognize that an affront to his Divine Majesty should be repelled with severity because the creature refuses to acknowledge and to act according to what he is—a dependent being. Because God owes us nothing, he is under no obligation to forgive, to consider extenuating circumstances, to overlook, or to give another chance. So in the case of the *non serviam*—"I will not serve"—of the rebel angels, we do not see the mercy of God.

In the case of man, God's mercy is apparent only after the whole human race is punished in Adam and after our first parents did penance for their personal sins.

When we reflect to what extent we are the recipients of the forgiving love of God, we should certainly be moved to gratitude. Moreover, when we take into consideration God's love for us and our knowledge of how we should act, then our offenses and negligences assume a greater unbecomingness, because ". . . to whom much has been given much will be expected."

My neglect to exercise my God-given stewardship is my defect, my sin. At the same time I am overwhelmed by the forgiving love of Almighty God. The secret of that love is Jesus Christ crucified. We read in Scripture, "By his wounds we are healed." And this healing is the forgiving love of God.

Fr. Evoy: God's way of dealing with the tragedy which is serious sin tells us much about him and about sin. To begin with, his love did not *have* to be a forgiving love. But Father Christoph has just stressed the fact that his love was and is a *forgiving* love. Why should it be such? Because, as we mentioned, love at its best looks primarily at the *needs,* not of the one loving, but of the loved one. As he looked at us, he saw a very great need for a loving forgiveness. When we sinned, we opened gaping wounds which we were utterly powerless to close. Here we get a glimpse of the enormity of sin, an evil so devastating that it can reduce the noblest member of God's visible creation to a state of pitiful helplessness. In sinning, man used his intrinsic freedom to enslave himself eternally. That fact tells us something about sin. And the fact of God's forgiving love tells us a great deal about God.

From the vantage point of needful sinners, I think that we might react to God's forgiving love with gratitude and appreciation. But were our response to God's forgiving love to go no further than gratitude and appreciation, it would be most unfortunate. In fact, I suspect that as women you are more aware than are men that such a reaction is indeed insufficient. Your very nature is to love a thoroughly good person when you really come to know that person. Why then should not this recognition of God's great goodness call up within you a personal love of God? I wonder if you would not agree that the answer seems to lie in how well you really get to know God. The lack of your love is not to be found in any lack of his lovableness. He is not only supremely lovable; he is infinite love itself. This is the reason why a correct knowledge of God's manner of dealing with our sins should increase our personal love for him.

Father Christoph mentioned the sin of the angels. When we reflect on any great sin such as theirs, it seems fitting for us to recall those oft-quoted words of Augustine. "There but for the grace of God go I." Sin is always presented to the sinner as attractive in some way. In fact, there is something about sin which can be strongly attractive even to an angel. Hence it would be a grave mistake for any of us to become smug, feeling we are immune to serious sin.

If sin can present itself as attractive to an angel, then can it not also present itself as attractive even to a saint? An understanding of the evil of sin by no means gives one a lifetime immunity to it. It is only realistic to say frankly that no matter how long we have been in religious life and no matter how free we have been of serious sins, we must beware of the pitfall of assuming that the grosser sins are impossible for religious. Satan still possesses the intelligence of an angel, and we still have the nature of fallen even though redeemed man. It is well indeed that the wise religious does repeat frequently, "There but for the grace of God go I." Nor ought we to even feel the inclination to look askance at those who are publicly recognized sinners, nor to feel superior to them.

The religious woman who views the whole matter correctly, regards the avoidance of sin in direct terms of her love. As a real woman she knows that she must love or experience within herself an emptiness. All you, as a woman, have to do is love with a true love. That is enough. If you continue genuinely to love God, you are without serious sin. In order to sin seriously you must really stop loving God. You might, indeed, dishonestly permit yourself to be deceived into an imitation of love. But the formula for avoiding serious sin is a simple one. It is thoroughly honest and genuine love. Love God and love all his sons and daughters. This means, first of all, really loving to the best of your ability every person who comes into your life.

By an extension it refers as well, in the wider sense of the word "love," to everything God has given you. Here of course I am referring to what you readily connect with St. Francis of Assisi who had a "love," in the sense of a grateful appreciation, for the birds, the trees, the flowers, and the entirety of God's visible creation. Must we still discover that the world God has made for man is beautiful, so beautiful that at times it hurts? When this world is rightly viewed, despite its trials and heartbreaks, there is something that grows on us, which is the joy resulting from loving God as we should. Our love for God transforms a world which seems drab to many into an iridescent place teeming with God's wonders. All the creatures in nature are God's ways of saying, "See, I love you." No matter how real and deep the hurts, the beautiful is still in the world. Our lives are by no means all joy and beauty, but God loves us, so all should be well with our world.

3 *Hell*

Fr. Christoph: At Mass we say, *Nobis quoque peccatoribus,* "and to us sinners," and the priest strikes his breast. This is not simply an empty gesture, for we are all sinners. We are reminded by St. Paul, "I chastise my body and bring it under subjection lest having preached to others, I myself become a castaway." There is something very objectively frightening in the Latin expression *corruptio optimi pessima,* "the corruption of the best always results in the worst."

Today for a number of reasons we are going to consider ultimate failure. First of all, because we ourselves can so fail. Secondly, because, recalling the example Father Evoy used, we know that the wound of any part of the body affects the whole; the failure of anyone to reach his final end in some way does harm to the Whole Christ. Our apostolic zeal should extend further than the salvation of our own souls, for we entered religious life to help Christ draw all things to himself. The possibility of hell for even one person should awaken in us true concern.

It seems to me that the knowledge we acquire as we contemplate hell ought to be of salutary advantage to us. If I know what will happen to a friend should he pursue a certain danger-

ous course, I will go out of my way to help him. If I see the
abyss into which a mountaineer has fallen, I will be better able
to warn others of the danger of falling. In the Exercises of St.
Ignatius, this meditation is posed very bluntly, i.e. if the love of
God does not have the power to make one live a good life, at
least the fear of hell will motivate him to avoid serious sin. Our
purpose in this meditation is not to frighten. Ours is not the fire
and brimstone approach to spirituality. But we should know as
many of the realities of the spiritual life as possible in order to
benefit from such knowledge.

Now we cannot gainsay the reality of hell. We would destroy
the very fabric of salvation history in the New Testament if we
were to ignore those instances where Christ spoke about hell and
its existence. In a recent controversial book written by a host of
Catholics on the problems of nonbelievers concerning the Catholic religion, one of the writers inveighs against the story of hell
because of its frightening impact.

If I tell a child, "Do not go near the precipice because you are
liable to fall," I am warning the child, not frightening him. I
would frighten the child if I held him over the precipice and
said, "I am going to let you drop!" When a parent tells a child
that fire burns, that poisons are dangerous, the motive is not
primarily to frighten him but to warn him. Should a father fail
to give this information to his child because he did not want to
frighten him, society would take a dim view of his paternal concern for his child's welfare.

We cannot sugarcoat reality. Since hell is a reality we have to
take it for what it is. Again, we are discussing hell, not primarily
out of fear, but rather out of love. We love God and we love our
own souls and those of our neighbors so much that we are going
to do everything we can to prevent even one of Christ's flock
from being lost.

Fr. Evoy: As Father Christoph said, when St. Ignatius placed
the meditation on hell in his Spiritual Exercises, he gave as the

reason for its inclusion that if one's love for God should prove insufficient motivation for living a good life, then his fear of hell might prove salutary. In a word, if people would not be motivated to lead good lives out of love, they might out of fear. When he gave that reason, I think he was talking to men rather than to women.

I doubt very much that many women are going to save their souls out of fear of going to hell. I would question that many women lead good lives because they are afraid not to. I would even suspect that those with such motivation are somehow not fully real women. For the most part, you simply do not frighten a real woman into being good. I think that the woman who does go to hell goes there because she is dishonestly trying to gratify herself, to live for herself alone, and endeavors not to admit that thereby she is doing wrong. A woman can know something is wrong in an intellectual way but disregard it in favor of gratifying a deeper, more desired inclination.

I am by no means implying that hell is meaningless to a woman. She well knows that hell is a fact, a revealed fact. It is, moreover, a fact that means a great deal to her, but not one which is likely to scare her into being good. It means immeasurably more to a real woman on the score that it threatens her with eternal separation from those she loves. This is really meaningful to her. Isolation, forever, from one she dearly loves, she understands immediately. In fact, the thought that should she go to hell she would be eternally walled off from those who are most deserving of her love would cause her intense real grief. Father Christoph mentioned the pain and suffering inseparably linked with hell. A woman is aware of these. Yet she is usually better able than a man to endure suffering if it is just physical suffering, so this pain does not compare for her with that of everlasting separation from those she loves or would want to love. It is this latter suffering which for a woman constitutes the tragedy of tragedies in hell.

Meditating on hell produces a further consideration which is of great importance to a real woman. She is well aware that love can never be a matter of bargaining. It is never a business of "I'll agree to love you if you will contract to love me." True love simply does not lend itself to "horse-trading." Yet a woman functions in a way which might at first glance have the appearance of bargaining. She never really loves a person without wanting a return of that love. And in this she reflects divine love. The infinite God, who loved her long before he established limits to contain the oceans, wants her to love him. As already mentioned, a genuine woman, when she comes in contact with a really good person, tends to go out to that person with proper love. Now, whether she recognizes it or not the great longing of her heart is to love God and to receive his love. In fact, it seems to be a violation of her nature for her to refuse to love one whom she comes to know as truly lovable.

With this explanation as background, we can focus on one of the most tragic aspects of hell. It is the fact that God continues to love the person who is in hell. The person in hell knows that God loves her and realizes moreover in a way words could never begin to portray that God is most worthy of all her love, that though she longs for his love, she may not accept it because she is no longer free to do so. In choosing serious sin and by dying in that choice, she has set herself forever against God. She has rejected him completely forever. Her persistent deep craving to love God must go frustrated for eternity. This, I think, is the worm that Scriptures says "dieth not." Though it tears her apart to do it, she continues through all ages to know that she can never, even for a moment, love him or accept his love.

A calm consideration of hell shows not only the fact of its existence but also the possibility that you and those you love could go there. Thus viewed, hell can become a very strong motive for your love of your fellowman. Because you really do care, you would not want another to go there nor would you want to go there yourself.

I am reminded here of one specific area of sin because of the sex differences it points out. Whenever a person of high moral principles becomes involved in an illicit love relationship with another person, there is a strong tendency to attempt to rationalize one's behavior. However, there is a difference in the woman's and man's patterns of rationalization. Frequently she will, to the extent that she is not a real woman, attempt to justify the relationship on the grounds that this is really love and therefore in a way not wrong. Moreover, she tries to tell herself that even if it is wrong she "doesn't care." She really does care and knows it is wrong but she is not woman enough to continue to look at it as wrong; she cannot easily live with it while admitting to herself that she is doing wrong.

The man in this kind of dishonesty would not be inclined to rationalize his own justification in this way. He finds himself needing to justify both to himself and to others his wrong behavior on the basis of what he insists are solid "reasons and arguments." At times the woman who has become thus involved will likewise enumerate "reasons and arguments" in defense of her behavior. The suspicion, however, is that in so doing she is repeating what the man has said, rather than what she herself has felt any need to bring forth. Perhaps what she accomplishes in repeating these "reasons and arguments" is not so much a logical justification for her behavior as a comforting support drawn from bringing him in, through his own words, to bolster her in the defense of her wrong behavior.

Fr. Christoph: From what Father Evoy has just said, there is an important lesson to be learned by women, including women religious. Because you are women, you must be sure you love in the right way. Then you do not have to worry about the consequences of your behavior because it will always be good. But there is a possibility of being led astray by your emotions. And because you are apostolically oriented women, you want to be able to recognize the pitfalls leading to serious sin and know exactly what hell is, so you will be moved to even greater zeal to preserve yourself from such an end and to help save others from this same tragic destiny.

Father Evoy gave you the clue to the real power of hell. The pain of sense, while you can appreciate it, seems in a certain way unimpressive. A woman can become largely inured to merely sensible suffering. But there is something that she cannot become accustomed to, and that is the pain of loss. "Our hearts were made for thee, O Lord, and restless shall they be until they rest in thee."

Hell is an eternal separation from God. The will is oriented by its very nature toward the good, and it will not be satisfied unless it possesses it. The will has had temporal experience of some aspects of that good and now it is forever denied the possession of that which alone can make it happy. Here in time all have the ability to love, and one of the things that enables you to go on living is the hope that you can love someone who will return your love. Because if you did not have the hope of sooner or later having someone—and I am not talking now about God—who can understand, appreciate, and love you, you would shrivel up and die, for true love tends to the other, craves acceptance. And in that acceptance the lover is content and happy. The soul in hell—if you can grasp this idea—is unable to love. Do you know what that means? Unable to love!

This experience, the inability to love, is so foreign to us that in great measure we have no idea of its meaning. When the soul is eternally frustrated by being denied that for which it is created, it still has the need to love but is absolutely unable to love. Worst of all, its hatred is turned back on itself because it must recognize that its present condition is of its own choosing.

Fr. Evoy: It is clear that the woman who enters hell will never love again. Love is neither received nor returned in hell. But this raises the question, "How can she live and not love?" In fact, it gives rise to the further question, "Can she actually call what she is doing in hell, 'living?'" I wonder if it would not be better called a "living death."

This does give us an insight into what hell is—a state of existence which might better be called a "living death" rather than "living." The woman in hell is in some ways like a robot, an animated kind of robot with feelings of pain, hate, and frustration, but not really alive in any positively vital way. Cut off at the point of no return from all those she could have loved, she is possessed of a most frustratingly imperious void because she can no longer let herself love and be loved. This is the emptiness that is to be hers for all eternity.

When she turns away from God, she turns her back on any further opportunity of loving. In so doing she denies her own nature, for in completely rejecting love she rejects everything warmly and tenderly womanly about herself. The best in a woman is necessarily that which is permeated by her love. In hell her need to give and receive love must forever go unsatisfied.

Hell is not a pleasant subject about which to think. Yet our Lord wanted us to know about the existence of hell. In the New Testament he repeatedly speaks of hell. His Church mentions it often in her liturgy. It is good for us occasionally to meditate on hell. It is also good for us to recall that God made hell, not for man, but for the fallen angels.

I prefer to take the position that the greatest number of hell's inhabitants are not men and women but angels. In fact, I like to think that there are few people in hell, and to the best of my knowledge this position is theologically sound. The reason I hold this is that hell can be earned only with malice, and I find so little unadulterated malice among people. This is by no means to maintain that men and women are incapable of malice. We know better than that. Though we find many human beings doing wrong things, I doubt that there is a great deal of malice. The point that moral failure can be culpable does not necessarily make it malice.

Besides, even when there appears to be malice motivating one's behavior, we cannot be sure that in God's eyes it is always such. An inadequate woman who appears to act out of malice may have been hurt. The pattern of her behavior may be to hurt back. God alone knows, however, whether her motivation is a cold, calculated, maliciously destructive thing. A woman's efforts to strike out at that which threatens her security often has the appearance of maliciousness. She can be spiteful, revengeful, or even hateful as she reacts to the feeling of having been scorned, humiliated, or at least threatened. Unlovely in her as are these reactions they are not necessarily of the evil cloth of malice. Since the Fall man has been inclined to evil. God, who neither is deceived nor makes mistakes, is the Judge. Only those who have earned hell go there.

Fr. Christoph: I think it is important to push this further. If there are people in hell, and doubtless there are human beings there, God still loves them despite the fact they are there, though they are unable to return that love. The apostolic aspect then of a meditation on hell should inspire you to a more generous living of your spiritual life. You know that the justice of God is tempered by the prayers, sacrifices, mortification, the loving service of those who pray for those who do not pray, who offer their lives to God for those who do not live for God.

If, as Father Evoy thinks, hell is not being peopled literally by hordes whom we see committing objectively serious sins, may it not be due to the fact that men and women with a real awareness of the nature of mortal sin—not a horror of hell, nor a fear of hell, but a horror of the eternal frustration of hell—are staying the hand of God? May it not be their total commitment that keeps God from saying, "Depart from me ye cursed into ever-lasting fire prepared for the devil and his angels"? Is it not in part our awareness of what can happen to a soul in hell that moves us to live for God, to pray, to give God a more generous service?

4 Death

Fr. Evoy: We are going to say something about what we might term the door separating our temporal from our eternal home. I am talking about the fact of death. Obviously, death is an experience that awaits each of us. No mere man has ever lived who by his nature was immune to the necessity of dying. There is no uncertainty about the fact of death; the uncertainty exists only with regard to the time and circumstances of death.

When our Lord pictured for us the Last Judgment, he addressed the group on his right hand as "good and faithful ones." In the word "faithful" there is for us a key to some profitable reflections on the subject of death. To begin with, look how our life races by. We find ourselves occasionally looking back and asking, "Where in the world did it go?" We might even begin to wonder of what value it was. Then we reflect on this one word our Lord addressed to those on his right hand. He called them "faithful." He addressed this word to those who had kept faith with him.

What is meant by "keeping faith"? It is nothing more nor less than a person's continuing to try, regardless of the failures, to live according to God's Commandments. The faithful person is the one who, despite the times he has fallen below the mark, has over the years endeavored to live so as to be pleasing to God.

But there seems to be a difficulty here. Did we not say earlier that each of us should seek to live from love? How then would we live from faith? There is no contradiction here. Faith is perfected in love. He who strives to keep faith with God is not for the most part motivated by what is tangibly present to him. He finds that it is rather a matter of living his life on the word of God. When our Lord said "Come to me all you good and faithful ones," he was speaking to those who, from a motivation of love for him, had built their lives on values they had accepted on faith in his word.

The longer we live here on earth, the more do we realize that the whole ultimate meaning of life is something that we take almost entirely on faith in the fact that God said so. There are no meanings which we can see visually. Through our physical sight we do not perceive God, we do not see the meaning of life, and we do not even see God's love for us. Our "seeing" the meaning of life and God's love for us is permeated through and through with the knowledge that wells up within us from the gift of our faith. These profound truths we accept ultimately because God revealed them to us. And our continuing to accept them and to live according to them, because they are divinely revealed, is indeed keeping faith with God.

Because you are seen by the world as religious, then just by keeping faith you are witnessing for God. You stand before your fellowman as a sign that the world, in its entirety, is from God. Your very presence among men is a symbol as well of the world's *for-God-ness*. In truly loving your neighbor you are telling him in unmistakable language that God loves him and that God's love for him is real—real because your love is real. Wherever you carry your love for man you become a reminder of God's love for man. When you really exist to others as you should, you are bringing them the evidence of the reality of his presence, of his goodness, and of his love.

Fr. Christoph: It may be well to emphasize a point that Father Evoy intimated but did not explicitly talk about: we must make an act of faith in the hereafter. We should constantly ask ourselves, "Why are we living like this?" If there were no hereafter, it would change our whole view of life. We might become existentialists in the Sartrean sense. We might come to subscribe to the position that we should eat, drink, and be merry, for we are going to be dead a long time.

On the word of God we make an act of faith that there is something beyond the grave. We do not see God. Neither do we see the hereafter; yet we know what awaits us there. The philosopher can prove the reality of the hereafter up to a point, but revelation has given abundant testimony to satisfy the man of faith. Christ said, "Come you blessed of my Father . . . good and faithful servant . . . because you have been faithful in a few things, enter into the joy of the Lord." But we may not enter into the joy of the Lord, for which death is the gate, unless we have been faithful here in time.

The only reason that I can face death with a smile on my face and a song in my heart is that I am not afraid of death. You have heard the statement "I am not afraid to die; I am ashamed to die." I am not afraid to die because "I know that my redeemer lives and that on the last day he will raise me up from the dead." Like St. Paul, one may say, "I desire to be dissolved and to be with Christ."

But I still might feel ashamed to die. This feeling could be in a faithful follower of Christ. Why might I be ashamed to die? Because it could be that as I look back and see the pattern of my life up to the present, I am conscious of some degree of infidelity in my stewardship. I could be worried about how faithful I have been.

Here we recall St. Ignatius's words, canonized by almost four centuries of use: "to use the things that come into my life insofar as they contribute to my end, and to abstain from their use insofar as they hinder me from attaining the end of my existence."

Some time in your meditations should be used to look retrospectively upon your life to see, in anticipation of the Final Judgment, what your reactions are to the stewardship of your life—the talents, friendships, charity, material and spiritual things. You have to give an account of everything and anything that has in some way touched your life. Fidelity, if it means anything at all, implies that you have been true to God. This means you have endeavored to be faithful to the divine will in your relationships to people and things. Accordingly if you have been reasonably faithful, then you may anticipate encountering death with no real need to feel ashamed.

Fr. Evoy: Recently I sat alongside a young man on a plane who had just been released from the military service the previous day. He was on his way home. His preoccupation, at that time, with the thought of going home is what now reminds me of what he said to me. Home had a meaning to him that stood out in contrast to the places he had been since entering the service. He had just been waiting, he said, all those months until he could get home. As he talked, it became increasingly clear that for him home was the place where things actually counted, where those who really mattered were, where his heart and his roots were, where his whole life found its center.

Should not this boy's plane trip remind us very much of death? Is death not just that? Is it not a going home? And to a religious especially, I think, is death seen as a going home. Going home is rich in meaning. Should not our sojourn here on earth be characterized by a longing for our eternal home?

The conversation I had with this young man reminds me of something else relevant to our present considerations. He fully

believed that our flight was taking him closer to home, but since
he did not once look out the window of the plane, he certainly
did not *see* that we were really headed in that direction. He was
told, when he purchased his ticket for our flight, that it was going
to take him homeward. He took the airline's word for it. This
is faith. True, it is natural faith. Nevertheless, taking something
as true on the word of someone else is an act of faith. It certainly
suggests the parallel in our journey toward heaven. We too take
it on faith, based on the revealed word of God, that we are, in
our journey through life, homeward bound.

Again the parallel with the young man on the plane is clear.
For him, home was first of all the persons there. Heaven, our
true home, means for us primarily the persons living there. Many
whom you have loved are waiting there for you.

Fr. Christoph: St. Theresa of Avila remarked that the thought of
life after death was of great value to her in the pursuit of her
perfection. Those of you who are familiar with her life know that
she lived in a turbulent period, and that the reform of Carmel
initiated by her caused her no end of heartache. When she was
depressed and found life difficult to bear, she thought of the far-
off land which was her heavenly home. These reflections made her
long to be with Christ, so much so that she said she thought that
the only people who really are alive are the people in Heaven.
In a very true sense she was correct, because they are the only
ones experiencing complete fulfillment in the possession of the
beatific vision.

The motto of Mary Queen of Scots was "In the end is my
beginning." Cannot each one say of her own death, "In the end
is my beginning"? Yet there are people who cling to life with a
zeal, anxiety, and effort which almost make you wonder if they
believe in a hereafter, and if they do, whether they envision any
happiness there. A man of faith, especially a religious, should be
able to say with St. Paul, "I desire to be dissolved and to be with

Christ." There is here no hatred of life nor fear of death but rather a realization of what lies beyond the grave for the good and faithful servant.

Fr. Evoy: God wants us to be happy. He placed within each of us an unquenchable thirst for happiness and he did not intend this urge to frustrate us. Neither did he limit all happiness exclusively to the life hereafter. There is simply no solid foundation for maintaining that we are not supposed to be happy here on earth. As a matter of fact, it is extremely difficult to think of anything which should be able to keep a Christian, as long as he is faithful, from being happy. On occasion, he may be sorrowful, disappointed and hurt, yes, but unhappy, no!

As real women you know immediately that unless you genuinely love those who count in your life, you are not happy. Happiness is an experience. I am quite sure that it would be impossible to define it adequately just because it is an experience and not some kind of idea. But even though it defies complete definition, it is possible for us to say something meaningful about it. It seems clear that a person is not happy when she fails to be what she should be—a real woman.

We understand immediately that our happiness here on earth is a good in its own right. We need sometimes to be reminded that it is also a foretaste of heaven. It is only a foretaste, because experience soon teaches us that without its relationship to eternity, it is never enough to satisfy the longing in our hearts. Happiness in this world is, without exception, something that rejects confinement completely to this life. We soon discover that our need to love will not be completely satisfied with limitation to the here and now. That is why, when rightly viewed, happiness in this world throws a new light on death. For happiness when seen in proper perspective says that death is the vestibule through which we must pass to arrive at that completion of flawless happiness for which there is a deep yearning in each of us. Death, then, can be the passover to indescribable happiness.

We have never actually discussed death with any human person who knows from experience what it is. Until we pass through it experientially, death remains for us an unknown. And just because death is such an unknown, some persons, regardless of how holy they might be, experience a real fear of it. This is a very understandable fear. When Father Christoph mentioned that death will not be encompassed with fear, he was by no means denying this. He was simply pointing out that even though there might be a natural fear of death, one who has kept faith with God will be enabled to cross bravely the threshold of death, with no trace of the paralyzing fear of those who in dying face a meaningless void. Even in the faithful person who is naturally afraid to die, there exists at the same time at another level of her experience the reassuring knowledge, from her faith, that it is all going to come out well. Though afraid, she surrenders bravely to God even in the surrender of death.

In accepting death you surrender to God in a magnificent act of trust, confident that after death you will be reunited with many of your loved ones, this time never again to be separated. But especially do you trust that you will meet the Three Divine *Persons* who created you out of love.

5 The Incarnation

Now it came to pass in those days, that a decree went forth from Caesar Augustus that a census of the whole world should be taken. This first census took place while Cyrinus was governor of Syria. And all were going, each to his own town, to register.

And Joseph also went from Galilee out of the town of Nazareth into Judea to the town of David, which is called Bethlehem—because he was of the house and family of David—to register, together with Mary his espoused wife, who was with child. And it came to pass while they were there, that the days for her to be delivered were fulfilled. And she brought forth her firstborn son, and wrapped him in swaddling clothes, and laid him in a manger, because there was no room for them in the inn.

And there were shepherds in the same district living in the fields and keeping watch over their flock by night. And behold, an angel of the Lord stood by them and the glory of God shone round about them, and they feared exceedingly.

And the angel said to them, "Do not be afraid, for behold, I bring you good news of great joy which shall be to all the people; for today in the town of David a Savior has been born to you, who is Christ the Lord. And this shall be a sign to you: you will find an infant wrapped in swaddling clothes and lying in a manger." And suddenly there was with the angel a multitude of the heavenly host praising God and saying, "Glory to God in the highest, and on earth peace among men of good will."

And it came to pass, when the angels had departed from them into heaven, that the shepherds were saying to one another, "Let us go over to Bethlehem and see this thing that has come to pass, which the Lord has made known to us."

So they went with haste, and they found Mary and Joseph, and the babe lying in the manger. And when they had seen, they understood what had been told them concerning this child. And all who heard marvelled at the things told them by the shepherds. But Mary kept in mind all these things, pondering them in her heart. And the shepherds returned, glorifying and praising God for all that they had heard and seen, even as it was spoken to them. (Luke 2:1–20.)

Fr. Evoy: The Incarnation is the central event in salvation history. In examining that history we are first of all confronted with the very basic question, "Why did God create you?" Certainly there could be no gain to God in such a creation. He not only possesses all being, he is infinite being. Why then did he create you? Fortunately he has not left us in doubt regarding his motivation. In Jeremias, God says, "I have loved you with an everlasting love, therefore I have drawn you, taking pity on you." His motivation for your creation was nothing whatever of gain or getting. It was a giving, for love is that way. So God created each of you to give you something, in fact, to give you everything, because he created you in order to share himself with you.

Now when he created you, God chose to endow you with a power of freedom so great that with it, if you so chose, you could do almost unbelievable things, including nearly incredible damage. Though but a mere creature, such is your freedom that you could go directly counter to the will of the Creator. You have the power to work the kind of destruction that you yourself could not mend or undo. And as you know this is precisely what our first parents used, or rather abused, their God-given freedom to do. They freely elected to do that which cut them off hopelessly from the goal for which they had been destined. They fastened the gates of Heaven against themselves and their descendants.

As salvific history proceeds, we find that God would not continue to permit those he loved to be eternally separated from him. "God so loved the world as to give his only-begotten Son." This restoration God accomplished at his own chosen time by sending his Son to become one of us. This unutterably wonderful event of God becoming a man is most difficult for us even to begin to understand. In fact, as you are well aware, it is a mystery. But though remaining a true mystery, there are some things about the Incarnation which God wants us to know. Otherwise he would not have revealed them to us. Let us look further into this glorious event of God becoming man.

The Second Person of the Blessed Trinity, while really distinct from the other two Persons, is nevertheless identified with the divine nature. It is a theologically correct statement that each of the three Divine Persons is the divine nature. This is why St. Cyril of Jerusalem could say simply that in the Second Person the divine nature became incarnate. Cyril was trying to make strikingly clear to us that God really became a man. The Second Person, the Word, took to himself as his own a human nature—a body and a soul, of which ever since he can say, "This is my own nature." Notice that he did not *become* a human nature, for he was and *is* a divine nature, but he now *has* his own human nature. It might be well to recall here that, by definition, a person who has his own body and soul is a man. The God-man fulfills perfectly this definition of man.

It is particularly difficult, I think, for us even to start to comprehend the depth of the descent that took place when the Creator stooped to acquire, as his own, a human nature. St. Paul attempts to express it by saying, "He emptied himself." To me it seems rather pointless to look for any adequate expression of the profundity of that descent because it is simply beyond the limits of our finite minds.

When I have tried to make it more meaningful to myself, I have hit on something that helps me. I think of it in connection with what, to me at least, is a particularly revolting member of the insect world—an earwig. If you have ever seen an earwig, I believe you will find no difficulty in agreeing that even its appearance is disgusting. I try to imagine what kind of love for other persons could motivate me, were such possible, freely to choose, while remaining the person I am, to lower myself into the body of an earwig and to live among earwigs as one of them. It is helpful because I can ask myself, "Did the Second Person do less when he emptied himself in order to become a man and dwell among men?"

Only divine love could have conceived and carried out such a lowering. The more we appreciate St. Paul's expression, "He emptied himself," the more we ask ourselves "Why?" The answer is simple. Were we to ask our Lord today, "Why did you become a man?", he would answer immediately, "Because I love you."

The Incarnation is unbelievably rich in matter for meditation. Take for instance the beautifully sacred scene of the young girl listening and replying to the angel as he announces to her that she is to be the mother of God. Little wonder that the Church has, over the years, referred to this event as the Annunciation. Quite simply stated, the Incarnation (and therefore our redemption also) by divine choice depended on the consent of one human being—a young girl whose name was Mary. God would

not have become man in her virginal womb without her surrendering words, "Behold the handmaid of the Lord, be it done
to me according to your word."

When we reflect that we could not have been thus redeemed
without the generous cooperation of Mary, it is well for us to
remember that this same redemption cannot be adequately carried out without the loving assistance of each one of us. God
has entrusted to us the application of the merits of his Son's
redemptive action. And so, God who "so loved the world as to
give his only-begotten Son" can continue that work of redemption, according to the divine plan which he has decreed, only if
and when we do our part.

As we study the Scriptural account of the Incarnation something else catches our attention. When Mary received the news,
she had a question. She asked, "How shall this be, since I know
not man?" In asking this question, she was by no means refusing
to believe what she had been told. But neither was she acting
like some poor little child, cringingly refraining from making a
very proper request for information that would enable her, operating as a real person, to cooperate more fully. Her question,
directed to the angel, stands out in stark contrast to another
question put to an angel.

Her cousin Elizabeth's husband, Zachary, also asked "how"
of an angel who had just announced to him that his wife at her
advanced age was going to have a child. But Zachary asked a
disbelieving "how" about what he had been told. He was asking, "How do I know that this is so?" In fact, he was demanding
a proof from God. This is something quite different from Mary's
inquiry. She had a proper difficulty; Zachary, an improper doubt.
The "how" asked by Mary was saying, "Since I do not see how
this can come about, would you give me some explanation?" By
giving her immediately the explanation, the angel confirmed that
Mary's question was wholly fitting and proper. On the one hand,
in the event of the Annunciation there is much for us to learn
about obedience. On the other hand, Zachary was punished for

asking his question, and therein also is a lesson about obedience.

Again it is well for you to note that Mary's complete surrender to God, which she expressed in her "fiat," is the prototype of your own surrender. It is the model for that which is most proper to your religious life. Under your three vows you have wholly surrendered yourself to God out of love for God. It is unfortunate if your own religious life is not actually saying, "Be it done to me."

It is not too difficult to see the divine wisdom in the fact that Scripture makes no mention whatever of Mary's external characteristics. Not once do you have a hint of such things as Mary's appearance, how she walked, or how she held her hands. This should save you from any preoccupation with attempting to model yourselves after her externally. To do so would be a kind of imitation of Mary that she would not want in you. She can well be your model for the important interior things which are hers because she is the perfect woman. Mary is your God-given example of proper attitude when she says, "Be it done to me according to thy word" and "he that is mighty has done great things to me."

In treating of our Lady we should make some mention of the Second Vatican Council's statement about her. That Council has said that Mary is to be treated *in* the Church. This is in no sense to be understood as detracting from her greatness. It is rather the matter of placing her in her proper context. A jewel shows best when placed in its proper setting. Mary should never be viewed apart from her son, and hence she should always be considered within the Whole Christ. The mother and son belong together. And even though we may not frequently make explicit reference to her, Mary will never be far from our thoughts during the following conferences as we strive to add to our knowledge of Christ. In fact, it is from Mary that we learn the valuable lesson that to get to know her son better is increasingly to enrich and personalize our love for him.

6 *The Visitation*

Now in those days Mary arose and went with haste into the hill country to a town of Juda and she entered the house of Zachary and saluted Elizabeth. And it came to pass, when Elizabeth heard the greeting of Mary, that the babe in her womb leapt. And Elizabeth was filled with the Holy Spirit and cried out with a loud voice, saying, "Blessed art thou among women and blessed is the fruit of thy womb! And how have I deserved that the mother of my Lord should come to me? For behold, the moment that the sound of thy greeting came to my ears, the babe in my womb leapt for joy. And blessed is she who has believed, because the things promised her by the Lord shall be accomplished."

And Mary said, "My soul magnifies the Lord, and my spirit rejoices in God my savior, because he has regarded the lowliness of his handmaid, for behold, henceforth all generations shall call me blessed, because he who is mighty has done great things for me, and holy is his name; and his mercy is from generation to generation toward those who fear him. He has shown might with his arm; he has scattered the proud in the conceit of their heart. He has put down the mighty from their thrones and has exalted the

lowly. The hungry he has filled with good things and the
rich he has sent empty away. He has given help to Israel
his servant, mindful of his mercy, as he promised our fathers, toward Abraham and his descendants forever."

And Mary remained with her about three months and
returned to her own house. (Luke 1:39–56.)

Fr. Evoy: Since our Lord had no earthly father, we would naturally expect him to resemble very much his sole human parent—
his mother. When we think of it, not only would we look for
a strong physical resemblance but we would also assume that this
mother and son would be alike in personality. After all, this is
the only instance in the history of the human race where a child
could and did choose his own mother. Christ would want to be
like Mary because he had singled out this admirable person
from among all women to become the most exalted and honored
mother of all time. So the old saying "like mother, like son"
would seem to have a special significance here. One way, therefore, of getting to know what Christ was like is to observe his
mother whom he resembled so closely. And happily, St. Luke
tells us a good deal about the mother of our Lord.

One thing that strikes us as we observe Mary immediately
after the Annunciation is her complete unselfishness. Look at the
situation as Luke presents it. Mary has just been told that hers
was the honor that would fulfill the longing of every woman in
the Jewish world. She is to be the mother of the Messias. This
she understands fully. She also is well aware that she has conceived her child in a miraculous way.

As women, would you not expect that her first motherly reaction would be, for a time at least, to find some little private
retreat where she could reflect on the inexpressibly glorious thing
that had just transpired within her? But if such an inclination
was hers, she did not act on it. She had just been told by the
angel that her cousin Elizabeth was soon expecting the birth of

her own child. Mary sensed immediately that under the circumstances Elizabeth would need both help and companionship. She could give her both.

I think that we can say with certainty that it never even occurred to Mary, now that she was the mother of the Promised One, that doing the chores in her cousin's house—washing the clothes, scrubbing the floors, cooking the meals and washing the dishes—would be below her dignity. These household chores are not generally rated at the top of the occupational scale. There is very little prestige in doing what could be done by hired help. Apparently that did not matter to Mary in the least. She had neither the inclination nor the time to compare what she was doing with what other women were doing. It is simply inconceivable to imagine that she would complain because she had to do these things which were below her dignity while other less honored women were doing more important things. It makes us wonder just which things are of greatest importance or whether things are really important at all in their own right, without any reference whatever to why they are being done.

There is another point here. Who told Mary to help her cousin? Did anyone suggest that she go? No one had to tell her. The motivation to go flowed right out of her love. Just as soon as she knew that Elizabeth needed her help, her love for both God and her cousin took her there. It is simply unthinkable that Mary would not have gone once she realized that one she loved needed her. In this—her genuine concern for and generous response to the needs of others—you would do well to imitate her, within the framework of God's manifest will for you.

Notice also that on her journey to Elizabeth, Mary took Christ with her. She was the first Christopher—the first Christ-bearer. Had she not gone to Elizabeth, our Lord would not at that time have reached either Elizabeth or her unborn son, John the Baptist. However, once Mary arrived at Elizabeth's house she did not have to concern herself with the matter of how she was going to make our Lord's presence effectively felt. He took care of that. Immediately he made his impact on Elizabeth and her son. Whether he used extraordinary means to accomplish this is not clear to us. And it really does not matter since what we see here is the fact that he makes use of whatever means are necessary. Only when ordinary means are insufficient, does he use extraordinary means.

Again, we observe that John did not, in fact could not, invite our Lord to visit him. One of the lessons here is that even when our Lord is brought to one who has not invited him, he is still effective. When you take him to those who have not invited him, who, in fact, may not even know him, he immediately becomes effective. It should be a great consolation to you that simply by really being what you are, genuine religious women, you take him with you wherever you go. Just by your being some place, he is also there. And when you really care enough about someone to get close to him, Christ will relate closely to that individual, who might not be aware that he is there. Whether this person you genuinely care about is a youngster in the classroom, an older person in the nursing home, a parent, or your fellow sister, you do not have to do our Lord's part; but he may never get close to any of these people unless you successfully do yours.

The redemption that Christ purchased for people is efficacious in direct terms of his contact with them. Christ still depends on people to take him to people. The true glory of your religious vocation is seen in your dedicated role of Christ-bearer.

Fr. Christoph: Almighty God uses human instruments to make his message known. In the instance of the Visitation, our Blessed Lady did what charity commended to her; there was an awareness of a need and the readiness to respond. She was not concerned about her own security or her own needs. She was not looking to her own convenience. How different this pattern is from that which we sometimes see in religion.

It is not difficult for a religious to settle for a pattern of observance in religious life by doing solely what she is asked to do when she is asked to do it. There is the danger of being almost selfishly concerned about the time she calls her own. The hours, the minutes, in a day that a religious can call her own are few indeed. It is easy to understand how she values them and wants to utilize them in her own way. Hence she could readily close her eyes to the daily, almost hourly, opportunities to serve others, and thus make her charity effective. And she can neglect these opportunities under the guise of religious observance. For example, she could use the excuse that she does not want to interfere in the office of another. The affairs of other sisters, she reflects, are no concern of hers. She can baptize and seemingly sanctify what is objectively a selfish attitude on the basis of her respect for the rights of others.

I might mention that often a good religious is prevented from offering her services to another because the other proves impossible to please or satisfy. Ordinarily, proffered assistance should be looked upon as a gracious gesture of help. But even a generous person may be hesitant and fearful about offering her assistance to an overexacting and overdemanding religious. So it is not surprising to find that some religious are left to do their tasks by themselves. They have no one to blame but themselves. They have driven away assistance.

The whole *raison d'être* of religious life is the charity of Christ binding individuals together, that they might cooperate mutually in the accomplishment of God's will through a particular kind of activity. What one can do well, two or three working together may be able to do ten times better. For in addition to their increased forces another important element is added: their capacity to perform more efficiently and effectively. It is not merely added help but also the enrichment flowing from the spirit of cooperation which makes for greater accomplishments. Religious ought to be very concerned about this spirit of helpfulness. Let me again remind you of the characteristic virtue of the Christian and *a fortiori* of the religious: "By this shall all men know that you are mine, that you have love one for another." This love must be unselfish—a love that does not hesitate to pay the price of inconvenience to self.

As Father Evoy very well said, "Who told Mary to go into the mountains to be with Elizabeth?" Was not her motivation the awareness that her cousin Elizabeth was aged, that she was doubtlessly without servants, that she needed the help of her kinswoman? Notice, there is no divine revelation to our Blessed Lady telling her to go to her cousin's assistance. Most often, as here, God uses natural means and expects one to respond with ordinary intelligence. Thus a religious ought not to wait for a divine inspiration before she is moved to offer help to her neighbor. This should be most true in her dealings with her fellow religious. Charity is, in a sense, before-handed because it perceives the need of another and is ready to help before the other even asks.

In her concern for her neighbor's needs the religious need not be nervously anxious to help. She should, however, show a willing disposition and a calm readiness to be of assistance. After all, charity is a virtue rather than a series of actions. Although a religious cannot always do what her charity suggests, she should be willing to be inconvenienced. Indeed, it hardly seems that one loves her neighbor if she helps her only when it is convenient. When she genuinely loves another, she is almost unconcerned about what is going to happen to herself.

The mother who dashes out in front of an automobile to rescue her child is not greatly concerned about the fact that she might be struck down. The mother who sits at the bedside of her sick child night and day is not gravely concerned that the rest which she normally needs is denied her. Her love makes her largely impervious to her own personal needs. Your love of your neighbor should make you at times more concerned about her needs than your own.

Sisters, you do not have to worry whether or not you are bringing Christ into the classroom, into the hospital room, the recreation room—into any situation in which you find yourself. If you are at your best—and you are at your best when you are a real woman, a Christian, and a religious—you cannot help but bring Christ with you. As Father Evoy has said, Christ does the rest. He takes over. So you do not have to be worried, for example, while visiting the sick, how Christ is going to be effective through you. You do not have to plan your remarks. Or in order to bring children closer to Christ you do not always have to tell them stories of his goodness. Just be your best self.

The selflessness of Mary should be mirrored in your attitude towards others. And this selflessness, springing from genuine love, makes you, like Mary, a Christ-bearer.

Fr. Evoy: We might consider further what it means to say that you bring Christ to the person with whom you come in contact. Actually, the only way many people know God is through you. Our Lord's reality comes through to them largely in terms of your reality to them. To the extent that they find you genuine and really caring for them, Christ comes to be experienced as a person by them. In view of this, can you not understand readily the remark of a person who, feeling he had been treated shabbily by a religious, shouted, "You can have your Christ. If that's the way he is, I don't want him." There is little point in trying to explain, later on, to such a person that the one who did this to him was not really Christ. This happens to be a tragic example of the most important fact that, with many people, as you go so goes Christ. In their eyes you represent him. Your religious habit proclaims that. In fact, it fairly shrieks out to them that you stand for and belong to God in a special way.

It is interesting to observe the first meeting of the home and school organization in any given school year. Many of the parents are then meeting the sisters for the first time. If you should happen to notice, some of these newcomers among the parents, especially the fathers of the children, are somewhat uncomfortable with you. Why? Is it because these men are always uncomfortable with women? I do not think so. Actually, I suspect you would find that many of them are never uncomfortable with other women. But in their eyes you are not just women. They do not know quite what to make of you. You are not like other women. To them, you are strikingly different. Were we to attempt to analyze just what is the difference in their minds, I think it would be that they regard you as somehow sacred, as belonging especially to God. There is some realization in most people that a sister is Christ's own and belongs to him in a special way. When these persons get to know you better, you become real women to them. As you become more real to them, Christ becomes more real to them too.

In a way, it should not be too difficult for you to appreciate the position of one for whom and to whom you make Christ real. I say this on the supposition that a number of you actually received your own experience of the reality of Christ, not directly from him, but through other persons.

Fr. Christoph: I would have my doubts that there is anyone of you who has followed her vocation on the basis of a direct divinely revealed personal invitation. Often enough, vocation comes through the mediation of men and women who bring Christ to others by their Christlikeness. The often repeated remark of our elders that when a certain priest came into the house it was like Christ coming into their home, was more than a pious expression. They were paying that priest the highest compliment. They were saying that he was Christlike. To be Christlike should be the desire of every religious. Hence wher-

ever your presence is felt, it should be not only you but Christ
too who is felt.

Fr. Evoy: You have evidence from your own experience, I believe, that the lovability of Christ is largely a matter of the
lovability of someone who had been to you a stand-in for Christ.
You came to know our Lord is lovable because his faithful one
was and is lovable. Christ has become a strong, kind, gentle man
largely because his friend—and your friend—is that way. It
should come as no surprise to your thinking then that Christ is
going to be just as real and admirable to some others as you are
to them—no more, no less. In this light, what a glorious privilege and grave responsibility are yours.

I feel that you will have no difficulty in agreeing that at the
Last Judgment you are going to have to give an account not
only for the evil you have done and left unconfessed but also
for the good you have failed to do. The Judge will address the
terrifying words "If you did it not to the least of these my little
ones, neither did you do it to me" to those who are eternally
lost. And hesitant as I am to say this, I have the feeling that
the Judge is going to be even more exacting on this score with
women than he is with me. Men are so often unobservant. They
just do not notice the needs of others as readily as do the women.

A man, at his best, may be allowed a certain lack of sensitive
perception, whereas a woman, at her best, would be expected to
notice when someone is really in need. In later reflections we
will consider at some length the Marriage Feast of Cana. Here
I wish merely to refer to something in it in order to exemplify
what I have just said. On that occasion, as it is described for
us in the New Testament, the greatest man who ever lived gave
not the slightest indication that he even noticed the great embarrassment of the newlyweds because they had run out of wine.
But the finest woman who ever lived sensed it immediately. And
no one is really surprised that this should have been the case.

In fact, we actually would have been surprised if our Lord had been aware of it and our Lady had not. So often Christ depends on women to point out to men the wants of his needy ones.

Fr. Christoph: I should like to have you reflect at least for some moments on one phrase of the Magnificat, the hymn of thanksgiving of our Blessed Lady after she was greeted by Elizabeth: "Because he who is mighty has done great things to me, and holy is his name." You can apply these words of our Blessed Lady, in a sense, to yourself. The whole history of your life can be summed up in these words: he that is mighty has done great things for you.

He has brought you into existence, at this time in history after the Redemption. He has given you, in baptism, the gift of faith. And wonder of wonders, without your deserving it, he has given you the gift of vocation. You look around and see even members of your own family perhaps who appear to be less undeserving of vocation than yourself. And yet you are the one whom he has chosen. For Christ said, "You have not chosen me, but I have chosen you." And you freely accepted this invitation. He has chosen you to be one of his special witnesses. God does not give you this grace without, at the same time, according you everything you need to fulfill your vocation most adequately. Since you are human and therefore essentially imperfect, your response to his invitation is going to be imperfect; your bringing Christ to your fellowmen is going to be imperfect. But you do your best.

Your vocation is a tremendous privilege to which you can never measure up adequately. But you can try. This is the optimistic realism of Ignatian spirituality.

St. Paul expresses the nature of your service to Christ in two simple words: "reasonable service." What God wants from you is not perfection. He wants this reasonable service—something which is within your competency to give, which takes into consideration your limitations, spiritual, physical, intellectual, moral.

This is what God wants of you and this is what your vocation should mean to you. Your norm is not what another is doing. You might know a sister who when she began her life in religion was more imperfect than you, but who seems now to have advanced so much. You are not envious of her. You are very happy that God has given her such grace and that she has apparently cooperated with it. The measure of your correspondence with the grace of vocation is simply what you have done with what God has given you, and not what others have done with the grace God has given them.

It is wonderful to reflect upon God's goodness to each one of you, to ponder the singular gifts he has given you, to rejoice in the greatness of your vocation. Nor should you forget that there is a unique relationship between God and yourself because of vocation. St. Paul reminds you that you are God's co-adjutors. God joins himself to you; he chooses to depend upon you, for you are an extension of Christ in the world. Yes, "he that is mighty has done great things to you."

Fr. Evoy: Father Christoph's point of avoiding any enviable comparison with another sister who might appear to have gone further under God's grace needs to be emphasized. From each of you God looks for the cooperation that you, and only you, can give him. He wants you to love him as a real woman and to take him to others. It is a temptation to say "If only I had been more generous" or "If only I had her gifts." It is vitally important for you to realize that he wants what is best, what the real you—starting from where you now are, regardless of what your past has been or of what other women might be doing—can give him.

In a word, what he really longs for is that you strive to give the best *unique* you to him and to his own. Your attitude ought to be "If this is what he wants, this is what I will give him." He can take care of all the failures of your past life. But without *your* present and future cooperation he cannot effectively help you to become the woman you should be. Every other consideration notwithstanding, the God-man greatly desires through your loving cooperation as a real woman to become present to others.

In conclusion, when in your dealings with other persons you are a real woman, whether or not you are aware of it, you are making an admirable presentation of Christ to them.

7 *The Nativity*

Now it came to pass in those days, that a decree went forth from Caesar Augustus that a census of the whole world should be taken. This first census took place while Cyrinus was governor of Syria. And all were going, each to his own town, to register.

And Joseph also went from Galilee out of the town of Nazareth into Judea to the town of David, which is called Bethlehem—because he was of the house and family of David—to register, together with Mary his espoused wife, who was with child. And it came to pass while they were there, that the days for her to be delivered were fulfilled. And she brought forth her firstborn son, and wrapped him in swaddling clothes, and laid him in a manger, because there was no room for them in the inn. (Luke 2:1–7.)

Fr. Evoy: It might be helpful here to recall the truth that God still speaks individually to you in and through his inspired word. Accordingly, whenever you are reading or listening to Sacred Scripture, you will gain much by reflecting that in it God is speaking to you personally. This means, therefore, that whenever you read or hear the inspired word you guard against at-

tending to it only as something God "once upon a time" said
to man. Instead, you cultivate the attitude of understanding it
as that which God is saying to you now.

Fr. Christoph: Moreover, according to the traditional pattern of
Ignatian contemplations you are to see the Gospel events, not
in the historical past, but in the present. This is especially true
in the revelation of Christ to man because he presents himself as
the example to imitate. "I am the way, the truth and the life.
Who follows me walks not in darkness" is what he actually says.
Until the advent of Christ, the good man wanting to live a life
that would merit an eternal reward had only the shadowy figures
and the words of the Old Testament prophets as well as the
dictates of his own conscience to guide him. With respect to the
specifics of daily life, much was left to his own interpretation.

But things changed with the coming of Christ, the God-man
who by his example—for he first did and then taught—shows
you how to fulfill the will of God in yourselves. Earlier you
were reminded that you have been given the precious gift of life
and that you are to reach your goal by the performance of deeds,
all of which would in some way contribute to your praise, reverence, and love of God. Now the question: How are you to live
your life? How are you to reach Heaven? You have the example
of Christ to guide you. Indeed, nothing less than the following
of Christ is called for now. You are to be at your reasonable
best.

How are you to be at your reasonable best as women, as
Christians, as religious? You are to imitate Christ closely. It is
true that you have your rules and constitutions and they spell out
the ideal religious of your community, but this ideal is drawn
from Sacred Scripture and especially from the life of Christ, the
model of every religious. In specifics, every once in a while you
have to go back to Christ's example in order to discover how
you must act. But you do not have to ask yourselves constantly

"How would Christ respond or how would he act in this or that circumstance?" After you have lived in religion, meditating on the life of Christ year in and year out, imperceptibly maybe, but nevertheless truly, Christ's way of looking at life becomes your way of looking at life, and Christlikeness becomes like a second nature for you.

Fr. Evoy: Against the background that in Scripture God is talking personally to you, let me enlarge somewhat on Father Christoph's remark that you are to be Christlike. When you are closely concentrating on Scripture, Christ is telling you, among other things, in what way he wants you to imitate him.

Take, for instance, the passage that we just read about the Nativity. One of the things God is telling you is that at times he wants you to do some things that are not derived directly from his expressed will. In fact, sometimes he wants you to do things that depend on the will of persons of little proven virtue, and even on those whose motives are more than a little suspect.

The example given in these particular verses is that of Joseph and Mary finding out that in order to carry out God's will, they were obliged to go to Bethlehem at a most inconvenient time. Why? Because a man named Caesar Augustus gave such an order. Why should they feel obliged to do what Caesar ordered? Because this man had God-given authority over them. What were Caesar's motives for ordering them to go to Bethlehem for the census enumeration? We do not know, nor do we need to be too interested in his motives. We certainly do not have to baptize his motivation in order to make a good case for the fact that Joseph and Mary owed him their obedience. They knew only too clearly that God's will for them was to obey every legitimate command of their superior. Among these commands was one to proceed to Bethlehem.

As women you would feel, I believe, that Mary's inclinations would have been to make detailed preparations so that every-

thing would have been suitable for the birth of her child. All
the little things would have been properly arranged as a woman
would wish them to be. But what is the actual situation? Someone in authority who does not know, let alone care, that she is
going to give birth to the Messias, decrees that they must travel
to Bethlehem immediately. So the will of God in this instance
consisted, not in doing what Mary would have desired, but rather
in living her "fiat." Here it happened to consist in *accepting*
what she did not like. The lesson for you is clear. God is telling
you that at times in order to do his will you will be called upon
to *accept* what you dislike.

Fr. Christoph: Father Evoy is implying that things do not always
come to pass the way you want them to happen. Among other
reasons for this is the fact that there are, at times, too many
variables involved. You cannot always have your own way, even
though to you it may seem to be the best way. In the historical
events surrounding the birth of Christ, a large number of people
and situations were involved. Yet if the events that took place
had not transpired, salvation history would have taken a different course. There is a lesson for us here. God is saying simply
that you must cultivate the spirit of indifference to the outcome
of events. Mary's indifference is first manifested in the Annunciation: "Behold the handmaid of the Lord. Be it done unto me
according to thy word." She was saying in effect, "I am here
at your disposition." In the Nativity she is living her "fiat" in
a concrete situation.

Fr. Evoy: Mary lived her "fiat," Sisters, throughout her earthly
life. As Father Christoph mentioned, she pronounced her "be
it done to me" at the Annunciation, but every day of her life
on earth she generously lived that commitment. The business of
having to leave for Bethlehem at a most inconvenient time was
but one of the earliest of many situations where she would pay

a great price for her original dedication. It is interesting to speculate how many of these costly payments Mary anticipated in her original "fiat." Certainly there were many which she could not possibly have foreseen. Take, for example, this one. When she made her "fiat," do you think that she knew that she would be asked to bring forth her son in an all-but-abandoned place? I think you would say, "Certainly not!" But not for a moment did she waver in the face of this unforeseen hardship; never did she entertain the thought of going back on her original commitment! But do you not think that she would have pondered *why* God had let this happen? I think she would have.

Fr. Christoph: Mary's "Why?" was not the complaint, "Why should this happen to me?" Rather, she was saying simply, "I do not understand." There is a big difference. It is not easy always to see the hand of God in the events that come into one's life. Nevertheless, one should take comfort in the encouraging words of St. Paul, "To them that love God all things work unto good." Here and now it may be difficult to see the workings of Divine Providence. Often it seems that things could be so much better. For example, if you had only a little more understanding from this person, or if only you had better health, more talent or a different talent, or if these present circumstances would change, it would be different. You do not live in a world of "if's"—if this . . . , if that . . . , if . . . ; you live in a world of reality, the same world into which Christ was born. Remember, Christ, the God-man, chose the circumstances of his own birth which seemed so unplanned. Father Evoy said that Mary did not understand why things had to be this way. But Mary knew the all-important fact that this was the disposition of Divine Providence for her at that moment.

Fr. Evoy: When we use this word "providence" I wonder if we do not tend to think of it as some kind of efficacious, impersonal, overall planning by God to keep disasters away from man and to keep the world running in reasonably good order. There is, however, nothing impersonal about God's providence. It is God's protective hovering over each of us. Clearly there are times when we do not see how events in our lives can be reconciled with God's loving concern. In the Nativity, God's loving care for the Holy Family and his special tender love for Mary were really present. But I wonder to what extent Mary and Joseph were aware of that love. Nevertheless, in their unhesitating obedience, they serve as models for us. They were in a position where they had to *trust* that his loving providence was present even though there was in their eyes little evidence of it.

In fact, I might go further and say it is not entirely inconceivable that Mary might have lovingly chided God, telling him how hurt she was at having to give birth to his Son in circumstances so naturally distasteful to her as a mother.

Besides, it is likely that all these happenings did not make a great deal of sense to her. I believe the explanation that Caesar had the legal right to make an accurate count of all his subjects would not have particularly impressed Mary. What did impress her was that it was God's will for her that she obey, and that was all she really needed to know in order to accept these circumstances.

Actually we have something of an advantage over Mary and Joseph in understanding the events surrounding the Nativity. Since we are not as personally involved in it as they were, we can view it more objectively. Moreover, we have a vantage point in time from which we can recognize that at Bethlehem God was teaching the world, among other lessons, that *things* are not of the first importance. Practically none of the things which they thought should have been there were actually present. God was saying in a way we should not miss that things are just not that important. What then is of great importance? Persons. God had arranged that three of the most important persons in the world,

Jesus, Mary, and Joseph, would be there in the stable. Is he not teaching most clearly that when the right persons are involved and when the relationships between them are right, things are of lesser importance?

Fr. Christoph: Humanly speaking, the pattern of events at the Nativity of Christ was not what Mary would have wanted, so she could have said to God, "This is not what I planned and I do not like it." Any mother in Mary's circumstances would have been humiliated and embarrassed by what happened. God does not expect you to deny your human feelings. What God is telling you here is that even though your feelings are very strong and very much in opposition to what you must accept, you are not to be governed by them. Mary is showing what this indifference means. Her son would say later, "Not my will but thine be done."

And here Mary, the handmaid of the Lord is discovering what her generous "be it done unto me according to thy word" really means. Mary could not *feel* indifferent to what was happening. But she did not let her feelings determine her behavior. You cannot, nor are you expected to, *feel* indifferent to all that happens to you. It may happen that you do not like a certain obedience that you have been given. You feel this but you do not allow yourself to become unduly upset because of what has happened. You accept this as God's will in your regard.

Fr. Evoy: Would it not be realistic to imagine that Mary might have *felt* like telling God, "I do not like any part of this arrangement for the birth of my son." Yet would it not be simply preposterous to think of her saying, "Because I do not at all like this arrangement, I won't do it. I will not accept it." That just would not make sense in our Lady. Do we ever wonder what God thinks of our response when we say, "This is not to my liking, so I am not going to have anything to do with it."

Fr. Christoph: You do not have to like it! If you did not have your likes and dislikes, your preferences, you would not be fully human. God knows that you experience these things, but you would be somewhat less than spiritual if you operated on the basis of your preferences. Even outside of religious life people have to develop and cultivate a praiseworthy indifference to things. The man who wants to get ahead works perhaps fifteen or eighteen hours a day for years. Would he not rather do something more pleasant, say, relax in the sun? Surely! But he has an objective so strongly desired that he lets nothing stand in the way of its achievement.

Our Blessed Lady had an objective: to do the will of God as she saw it. This meant everything to her. And you, as religious, by your vows have said, in effect, "Be it done unto me according to your word." This does not mean that you may not express preferences in the carrying out of difficult assignments. Nor does it mean that you may not have strong feelings with respect to health, talent, opportunities, acceptance by others, and the like. You would be less than human if you did not have such feelings and preferences. But you would not be true to your vocation if you allowed them so to affect you that you could not carry out unpleasant assignments.

Fr. Evoy: This would be taking the position that you do what is demanded of you if and when you like it, and if you happen not to like it, you do not do it. Such a position would simply be unthinkable for Mary. Why should it not be equally unthinkable for you? In taking your vows you said, "Be it done unto me according to thy word." There was no mention there of likes or dislikes. Any way you correctly spell out the meaning of your vows, it always comes out as a complete surrender to God. You have simply said that whatever God asks, with his help you will strive to do. This does not mean, let me emphasize, that you have to like it. Taking vows does not change your nature. You are not long in religious life before you find yourselves with a strong feeling against some obedience. You might have said truthfully more than once that you did not like something, but this was not saying that you would not do it.

Fr. Christoph: We are inclined to react to pain or sorrow with agonizing silence, tears, or cries; to joy with a smile and expressions of delight. You are not expected to suppress or rid your life of these very human reactions. God says simply that you may not live according to your feelings. Even in something as ordinary as getting up in the morning, you may feel reluctant to rise at the appointed time. This is how you feel. It is not your feelings, but what you want to do, that should govern your behavior. So you normally get up simply because you want to do God's will even in this little matter.

Fr. Evoy: I would assume that Mary probably talked to Joseph about her feelings of disappointment evoked by the circumstances surrounding the birth of her son, since when two people genuinely love each other, they can communicate about everything. Not for one moment, however, would I imagine that she did so in such a way that he felt she was blaming him. She knew that Joseph was already pained that he had not provided better for her and her son.

But I think she would have needed to talk to someone whom she could trust and Joseph would be just that someone. I feel that along with other things, she would want to tell him how bewildered she was that God should have permitted these events to happen. But Mary would not have been complaining. She would have just been expressing her feelings. And I suspect that Joseph, too, would have been relieved to talk about these things associated with the Nativity.

Sisters, there will be times in your lives when you will be hurting and will need someone to talk to. Fortunate are you if then you will have someone to whom you can freely go. On occasion, you feel the need to confide in another person. As long as you show real consideration within the framework of religious life for this other person, it is entirely proper to place such confidences. Often your need is more to find someone who will understand than it is to get answers to your problems.

Fr. Christoph: I would like to emphasize the phrase Father Evoy used, *"if you can find someone."* We all stand in need of some of Niebuhr's "listening love." I am sure our Blessed Lady found the consolation of "listening love" in St. Joseph. Our love, too, should often be a listening love.

St. Ignatius suggests that in your contemplation you make the scene present to you—to see, to watch, to listen. Look at the Nativity scene again. This is your first contact with the Word made flesh, with him who says, "I am the way, the truth, and the life," and "Who follows me walks not in darkness." Surely you must be struck by the indifference of Christ to material things. He even chose the less pleasant. Suffering is Christ's lot from his birth.

Look again. There is nothing to suggest divinity. Yet our response should be an act of faith in the divinity of Jesus Christ whose Godhead is certainly not visible. This act of faith has to be vital enough to enable us to see not only the divine in the infant in the crib, but to see the divine in everything that comes into our lives. "He came unto his own," as St. John says, "and his own received him not. But to as many as received him he gave the power of becoming sons of God; to those who believe in his name."

Fr. Evoy: Because you are women, you have some understanding of how our Lady felt about having to give birth to her son in a stable. In your meditation, you might even eavesdrop on her conversation with Joseph, and let yourself really experience the feelings which spontaneously arise in you as you contemplate the scene.

8 *The Finding in the Temple*

And his parents were wont to go every year to Jerusalem at the Feast of the Passover. And when he was twelve years old, they went up to Jerusalem according to the custom of the feast. And after they had fulfilled the days, when they were returning, the boy Jesus remained in Jerusalem, and his parents did not know it. But thinking that he was in the caravan, they had come a day's journey before it occurred to them to look for him among their relatives and acquaintances. And not finding him, they returned to Jerusalem in search of him.

And it came to pass after three days, that they found him in the temple, sitting in the midst of the teachers, listening to them and asking them questions. And all who were listening to him were amazed at his understanding and his answers. And when they saw him, they were astonished. And his mother said to him, "Son, why hast thou done so to us? Behold, in sorrow thy father and I have been seeking thee."

And he said to them, "How is it that you sought me? Did you not know that I must be about my Father's business?" And they did not understand the word that he spoke to them.

And he went down with them and came to Nazareth, and was subject to them; and his mother kept all these things carefully in her heart. (Luke 2:41–51.)

Fr. Evoy: The implication in the Gospel account just read is that this was the first time Jesus had gone up to Jerusalem with his parents. The reason he did so at this time was that he had just turned twelve years of age. From the beginning of his thirteenth year every Jewish boy was subject to the Law. The Law was not intended to bind its maker, the God-man. But our Lord submitted to it in order to teach us a valuable lesson.

In a sense the Law is similar to any system or order of things. Take, for instance, the horarium of a religious community. Such an overall ordering is designed to govern the behavior of the community. We readily understand that some general set of regulations and rules is required for any large group of people living together. This is certainly true of religious life. Without such regulatory framework things would approach chaos.

While such a general ordering is required for the good of the house, it certainly does not follow that every detail of the horarium is at all times suitable to each member of the group. Human nature being what it is, such simply cannot be. The Church has never said that such a body of regulations is in every instance tailored to every person regardless of the situation. In fact, one could not prudently hold this to be true. Take, for instance, the matter of the time of rising in a religious community. Let us say the rising hour is five o'clock. One sister might not be able to get to sleep until one or two in the morning. Should this happen repeatedly in her case, on what basis could it be maintained that daily five o'clock rising would be admirably suited to her? It simply would not be so.

Because such instances of unsuitability could be multiplied, it must always be kept in mind that religious rules, though sanctioned by the Church, are man-made and hence subject to all the limitations characteristic of human foresight. It is of the utmost importance that superiors and subjects alike be ever mindful of this.

Whenever, then, a rule or regulation works an unreasonable hardship on a given religious, what is to be done? The religious person concerned might choose, like the Child Jesus going up to Jerusalem, to submit herself to this law. However, this would be permissible for her only if she judged that such submission would in no way lessen the effectiveness of her work for Christ. Unless she felt this to be true, she would be obliged in conscience to bring the hardship to the attention of her superiors. In other words, should she judge that she needed an exemption from the rule or regulation, she would have an obligation to present her reasons to one or more persons in authority. Superiors, on their part, should not only be willing graciously to grant such an exemption but should sincerely want to grant it whenever they would become aware of a sufficient reason for doing so.

Fr. Christoph: Let us presume that Father Evoy is the Chairman of the Psychology Department in a university. A student comes to him with a problem, and Father grants him a waiver on a departmental requirement. Suppose now that the Dean says to Father Evoy, "You cannot do this because you are not following the catalog in this matter." Father Evoy might very reasonably reply, "Then you do not need a chairman of this department. All you need is a clerk to read the catalog." The chairman should have the authority to grant an exemption to a departmental requirement in a given case. This is why we have people in charge.

People are put into positions of authority in religious life, not to police the institution, or merely to see that the rules are kept, but among other things to be able to interpret the rules in specific instances and in any *human* way.

I would not want to give the impression to anyone that rules are made to be broken or that there should not be rules and

regulations in a community. Guidelines, such as rules for behavior, are not unique to religious life but are essential to any
type of organized living.

The structure of the Jewish Law was rigid, making few allow-
ances. So when Jesus was twelve, he went to the temple as was
prescribed in the Law. While, as Father Evoy said, he was not,
strictly speaking, subject to the Law, nevertheless others did not
know this and in order to avoid scandal Christ submitted to the
letter of the Law. So also in religious life, when you are actually
excused on occasion from the observance of a particular rule, you
may choose to observe it externally, out of consideration for
others.

Fr. Evoy: In this Gospel account there is a great lesson for us
regarding the proper exercise of authority. Notice that there is
not the slightest trace here of any overprotection of the Child
Jesus by Mary or Joseph. In fact, we are somewhat surprised at
the trust they placed in him. They simply took it for granted
that this twelve-year-old knew what he should do. Once they were
satisfied that he understood what he was to do, they assumed he
had both the ability and the sense of responsibility to do it. This
is trust. There is no indication here of a hovering over him to
protect him from making mistakes. They knew that the Child
Jesus understood that they were to leave for home with the caravan. There is no evidence of any checking or making sure that he
knew in detail how to go about the return trip. What a striking
lesson in the exercise of authority God is giving us here. It ex-
emplifies real trust on the part of the person in authority and
real responsibility on the part of the subject.

Clearly, it was a shock to both Mary and Joseph when they
discovered that Jesus was not in the caravan. And did they resolve then and there never again to trust him? I wonder if that is
not what we might have done? On the face of it, Jesus had failed
his responsibility and violated their trust. On the *face* of it he

had. Mary and Joseph did not understand. They knew that he had not done what they expected, but they did not understand why. Nevertheless, they did not jump to any conclusions. When they finally found him, Mary *asked* him why he had done so to them. In so doing, she was not leveling an accusation. She was seeking information. Jesus expressed his surprise that she asked. It was an embarrassing moment, I think, for both Joseph and Mary.

Apparently Jesus hoped that when they noticed his absence, they would simply assume that because of a higher obligation, he was unable to abide by their wishes. "Did you not know that I must be about my Father's business?" Jesus was indicating to them that they should not have been deeply troubled by his absence. He was saying, in effect, that he had simply assumed that they trusted him completely, which would include the fact that since he had not joined the caravan, he would return as soon as he was free to do so. His implication was that they should not for a moment doubt that he could explain satisfactorily his failure to join the caravan.

What a lesson for us, especially those of us who are or will be in positions of authority! As we contemplate this scene, we notice in Mary and Joseph not a trace of the attitude "You failed to do this, therefore you were disobedient." There is absolutely nothing here of his being accused and found guilty, let alone sentenced without so much as a hearing. In fact, one gathers from Mary's words that she knew her son would have a good reason for the suffering he had caused them by his apparent disobedience. What a magnificent example of trusting another even when there seemed to be a lack of sufficient grounds for such trust. And Jesus, in his turn, remained fully trustworthy even while giving the external appearance of disobedience.

Fr. Christoph: Now let us put this in the framework of religious discipline. In a sense, Jesus chided his parents when he asked them why they sought him. Did they not know that he must be about his Father's business? They should have known that he would needlessly do nothing to hurt them, that he would not be disobedient. In a religious community the presumption, unless there is real proof to the contrary, should be that the behavior of a subject can be completely justified once all the circumstances surrounding this behavior are known.

So often judgments are made without the proper facts. A superior need never scruple if she presumes that every subject acts reasonably and out of good motives. This kind of trust obviously calls for responsibility on the part of the subject. She must be genuinely trustworthy. I can understand a superior being tempted to lose confidence in some of her subjects if she has been deceived by several members in a small community. But antecedent to any such verifiable evidence, the presumption is that everyone in her convent is trustworthy.

Fr. Evoy: I think one point needs to be stressed here. Could you for a moment imagine Mary and Joseph, when they finally found Jesus in Jerusalem, saying to him, "That is the last time we ever trust you out of our sight. We trusted you and see what happened." Even after Jesus had explained, Mary still did not fully understand why he had not been with the caravan. But even though she failed to comprehend it, could you conceive of her resolving never again to trust him to do something by himself? However, how ready are we at times to resolve never again to trust one who has failed even once to measure up to our expectations.

Fr. Christoph: Religious life has come to a very sad state in any community where one offense against a rule renders a sister untrustworthy. After all, many factors enter into behavior; hence superiors may err in making a judgment. Moreover, superiors should be vigilant lest they make regulations based solely on the atypical behavior of a few members of the community. But religious subjects need to be reminded repeatedly that theirs is the corresponding obligation of honoring the trust placed in them by their superiors. This is a two-way street. For, just as our Blessed Lady and St. Joseph did not show lack of trust in Jesus, neither did he throughout his childhood show himself to be untrustworthy.

Sisters, trustworthiness has many ramifications. For instance, each religious bears a responsibility for the reputation of the entire community. A community may pay dearly for the imprudence of even one religious, since externs tend to judge the group by the behavior of the individual. Hence, at times, what would be acceptable conduct in a lay person would not be so in a religious.

Sometimes young religious complain of surveillance, and rightly so. They also resist what they regard as the unreasonable curtailment of their activities. Often enough, such vigilance and restrictions by superiors spring from the judgment that youth lacks experience and may act imprudently. Superiors wonder whether these subjects are sufficiently mature to be permitted this freedom of action. Superiors often find it very difficult to work out this relationship of trusting subjects because, among other things, they detect faulty premises underlying the behavior of some of their religious subjects.

For instance, the reaction of some religious today to their rules and the justification for their conduct is not infrequently the timeworn expression that the rules do not bind under sin. While this may be canonically and morally correct, it hardly represents the ascetical ideal. By profession and especially by the expressed words of Canon Law ". . . . all religious, superiors as well as subjects, are bound not only to observe faithfully and entirely the vows they have taken, but also to order their lives according to the Rules and Constitutions of the institute to which they belong, and thus *tend to the perfection of their state*" (Can. 593).

This means that religious have freely assumed the obligation of striving for their perfection. It is therefore out of keeping for one to justify her conduct on the basis that what she is doing is not sinful.

In the Gospel episode we are considering, Jesus is teaching still another lesson—the need of a becoming detachment from family and kin. When you entered religious life, while you did not cease to be a member of the family that nurtured you, you had to be detached enough from parents, brothers, sisters, and other relatives so that they would not hinder you from being about your "Father's business." This is your primary commitment now.

What happens to the spirit of community if at every opportunity a religious is, by preference, with her blood relatives rather than with those who constitute her religious family? Allegiance to one's fellow religious in no way detracts from proper filial piety. To love those closely related by ties of blood, to be interested and concerned about their welfare, is natural. Indeed if one has no such interest, it might be regarded as unwholesome. But, as in all other things, this interest should be well ordered and subordinated to one's basic commitment.

Fr. Evoy: Christ's words "I must be about my Father's business" give the key to the right viewpoint in this matter of relationship to one's family. The main business that each of you as a religious must be about is not primarily concerned with your family. It is, however, intimately linked with your religious community. Indeed, often it is precisely because you are a member of the community that you engage in your more important undertakings. Father Christoph's point is not that you should neglect your own family, but that were you to make them and their welfare your principle concern, it would mean an absence of proper perspective. On the other hand, you should always care, and care deeply, about your family and your close relatives.

Fr. Christoph: Every religious could admirably make the words of Christ "I must be about my Father's business" her motto. To gain the whole world for his heavenly Father is the work to which Christ constantly addressed himself. And there is an obediential disposition in Christ to carry out this redemptive undertaking always.

Any religious community must put some limitations on its activities. No community is able to do all the good that should be done. Thus there are a number of good works which do not happen to be within the scope of your community's commitment. In fact, there are doubtless some good works which may not be the proper activity of any existing community. In the interest of intelligent planning each community must limit its objectives. This your community has done.

You may feel attracted to some field of social service, but if this does not happen to be within the scope of your community's undertakings, it would not be a part of your Father's business to be done by you. A truly zealous religious may see many fields ripe for harvest. She may become impatient, for instance, because her community is not establishing a school for socially deprived children in Alabama. However, superiors have come to the conclusion that this is not a feasible apostolate for the community at this time, and she submits herself to this judgment.

Fr. Evoy: No community can do all the good that needs to be done in the world—a point that Vatican II teaches forcefully. Neither can any one religious do all the things that pertain to the interests of her Father's business. A given community undertakes a limited number of works in a limited number of places. These works are regarded as proper to the community in question. Therefore, a religious takes care of an area of her Father's business which is within the framework of the work of her community.

This is not to deny that a sister might think it advisable to establish an institution in Alabama. But she recognizes it is highly unlikely that this will be undertaken by her community.

The number of possible good works to be done approaches the infinite. There may be a need for more leper colonies, but others will have to take care of that part of the Father's business. This is not to be understood as ruling out all possibility of change in the undertakings of the community. If a sister were convinced that it would be better for her community to curtail or even to discontinue a present work or to venture into a different field of work, she would be morally free to suggest or even recommend such changes to those in authority. Meanwhile, being "about her Father's business" means doing the best she can in one or more of the works which her community is currently undertaking. Hence for her, the business of her heavenly Father is bringing Christ to *all* those with whom she presently lives and works.

It is well to point out that when religious find confinement to specific works irksome and feel, moreover, that their zeal is being unreasonably restricted to the works of the community, there might be grounds for suspicion of self-deception. I am concerned here especially with what has been called the heresy of activity. This is the unsound position that a person's holiness consists primarily in activities. Even though a sister belongs to an active rather than to a contemplative community, the true value of her work is certainly not to be measured quantitatively either in the magnitude or the number of her apostolic undertakings. The statistical attitude that the more things one does the better and the more pleasing it is to God is not only fallacious but perilous. In fact, the members of a community can be spread so thin with a proliferation of works or they can be burdened with work that they do not have sufficient time even to pray.

Fr. Christoph: It is obvious that your worth as religious does not come specifically from teaching, or nursing, or administrative activities, or the like. Lay people can be hired to do these things efficiently. Your value as a member of a religious community comes especially from the fact that you are a manifest extension of Christ in the specific area of the world in which you are active.

Fr. Evoy: As religious, you provide a social reminder of the call of all men to holiness. At the same time, many of the things done in the community would not appear to be very important. Among the really important things done in religious life can be those that would receive very little attention in the world. For instance, one sister who is seriously ill lives her love for God by cheerfully bearing her painful sufferings. Other sisters can live a life of love toiling in the kitchen, the sacristy, the laundry, or doing the house work. Who is to say that these dedicated activities are of lesser importance than those which receive more public recognition?

Fr. Christoph: A sister came to me and said that she felt that our Blessed Mother would not have discussed the disappointment she felt at Bethlehem with St. Joseph. I suppose this sister would feel that Mary would not have spoken to St. Joseph about her anxieties while looking for her divine son in the temple precincts either. This would have been true were not St. Joseph the man that he was. We have from the beginning been stressing the true nature of the real woman in these conferences. Now it is a tremendous tribute to the loving understanding of St. Joseph that Mary would know that he would want to share with her not only her joy but her pain as well. Communication is as essential a part of love as are trust and understanding. True communication between Mary and Joseph would have to include, therefore, the sharing of pain and suffering.

The point should be made that God did not deny painful experiences to the two whom he loved so dearly. To begin with, at Bethlehem our Blessed Lady and St. Joseph experienced keen disappointment. Certainly, the flight into Egypt was in many ways a painful undertaking. And here, while searching for our Lord in the temple, they were saddened and worried. Later Mary was to be left a widow. And even Christ, in a physical sense, would leave her. There was no miraculous protection from the disagreeable and the undesirable. It would not be right to expect God to spare you all suffering. But as he gave Mary and Joseph the grace and strength to endure life and its problems, so too does he give you the grace and strength to endure the trials that come into your lives. Later on would he not say to St. Paul, "My grace is sufficient for thee"?

"Mary kept all these things carefully in her heart." She wondered why God permitted these sufferings but she wondered within the framework of God's love, his tender care, his divine providence. There was no questioning that love. If you reflect in this same spiritual manner, sooner or later the message will come through to you from Christ as indeed it did to Mary. St. Catherine of Siena on one occasion was sorely tried by severe temptations. After the struggle was over, she complained to our Lord, "Where were you when I needed you the most?" And Christ answered, "I was with you. Without me you would not have overcome." God always gives the grace one needs to fulfill his will. This is God's way of showing his love.

Fr. Evoy: I should like to suggest one last consideration. According to Scriptural scholars, "grace" in the statement "He increased in wisdom, age and grace before God and men" does not mean actual or sanctifying grace. It means graciousness. And it seems to me, Sisters, the lesson here is particularly relevant to you as women. For a real woman is truly gracious.

9 *The Hidden Life*

Fr. Christoph: "And he went down to Nazareth and was subject to them." Two brief remarks are all we find in Scripture to describe the life of Christ from his twelfth to about his thirtieth year. In about thirty words Sacred Scripture accounts for two-thirds of the life of Christ. Some of you are less than thirty years of age and you would dislike to have your lives up to the present written off so briefly. I should like to have you reflect for a few minutes upon three points that these two short verses call to our mind: the example of Christ's hidden life, the community spirit at Nazareth, and Christ's life of obedience there.

First, take the example of Christ's hidden life. It is natural to want to be known. We are all at least to some extent flattered if our names are mentioned in the Chronicles of the house, if our pictures appear in publications, or if commendatory remarks are made about us by people whose opinions we value. No one naturally wants to be unknown. But in the normal life of the ordinary individual the occasions for public notice are, for the most part, limited.

The life of the average person is rather unspectacular. And no less unspectacular is the life of the average religious. Notice I did not say "drab," because we ourselves are to blame for any element of drabness in our lives. Our lives can and should be exciting. Drabness is an implicit admission of a lack of proper motivation. The generous following of Christ should be a truly vital experience.

I said a moment ago that the average individual's life is unspectacular. I think this is one of the reasons why Christ deliberately chose a life, the greater part of which was not spectacular. He chose to live in the little province of Galilee, in the little town of Nazareth, hidden away in the hills, commonplace in so many respects. Yet, this is the place chosen by the Son of God. Christ is teaching us that we should be willing, out of love, to do our best even though there would be no publicity attached to our efforts.

This lesson is sorely needed today when celebrities employ public relations experts whose sole role is to see that they receive a good press and much public notice. These are the last things we should be seeking. We should cultivate a certain contentment with whatever obscurity may be ours. If today I am appointed to assume a prominent role in the community, I accept it with true humility. If tomorrow I am back in the "ranks," I accept with equal grace.

There is a normal desire on the part of all of us, to receive recognition for our achievements. We tell ourselves that we act out of the love of God, and this should be the case, but we may be moved more by self-love. If the saints would confess at times, "There is so much of me in me," we have to be vigilant lest we deceive ourselves in the matter of our motivation. Discernment is called for. We should recognize that, by our profession and the circumstances of our work, we may be committed to the hidden life. If so, it will be difficult to live such a life unless we see its value through the example of our Lord. One might be tempted to think that Christ wasted his time in that insignificant town. In fact, the contempt with which Nazareth was held was expressed in the words of Nathanael, "What good can come out of Nazareth."

Again, one might maintain that Christ could have made better use of his time by exercising his apostolate out among the people. In somewhat similar fashion a younger religious might think, "Why do they not, at this time, let me get involved in this social movement? Why do they not let me write for publication? Why do they not let me get into a classroom?"

It is simply not true that a religious has to be formally employed in the works of mercy in order to be doing God's will. A community wisely requires in its members adequate preparation for the active apostolate. Just as Christ was doing his Father's will all the while he was at Nazareth, so too the religious ought to be confident that she is doing his will when, with fidelity, she performs her assigned tasks. At Nazareth, Christ put the stamp of his personal approval on that which was, in fact, unspectacular. And since the life of a religious is so often made up of the unspectacular, it helps to recall that Christ put a high value on such a way of life.

I should like to develop the second consideration, namely, that Christ lived a life of community in Nazareth. We call it the Holy Family. Reflect upon the way the Holy Family lived: the spirit of charity that reigned in that home, the mutual help, the subordination of the God-man to his creatures who were inferior to him, the sense of oneness.

Each sister must look at herself and say of the community, of the house in which she lives, "I have an obligation to reproduce as much as possible Nazareth and the type of community that is symbolized by the Holy Family: a life of charity and a life of cooperation, a life of unity that includes everyone. Is this not what we mean by *community?* It is a problem to achieve this, especially in small communities. Everybody must be *dedicated* to charity in a small house. I say this of every house, but in a small house charity must include everyone from the oldest to the youngest sister; all must feel they are part *of* and not apart *from.* I am sure that the conversation in the home of the Holy Family was not necessarily always oriented towards Christ.

Your constitutions say that everyone should be included in recreation, and that conversation should not be so specialized that it excludes some of the sisters present. This regulation should be taken in the sense in which it is intended.

Your activities at school, for example, may have many interesting insights, humorous asides, and even experiences that would be helpful to the other members of the community. So you talk about those things. If the housekeeper does not know the pupils in school, this should not prevent one of the sisters from telling a story about Johnny Jump-up that is very edifying or amusing. It is permissible to talk about your students in that way. You always have an obligation to refrain from talking down to those sisters who are not associated with the school. On the other hand, sisters who are not directly connected with the school have a responsibility to show some interest in the pupils and school activities. It works both ways.

Thus it becomes possible for the small community to be welded together in fraternal unity. Recreation, common tasks, and community concerns should embrace all of the members of a given community. Only in this way will there exist the spirit of cooperation and fraternal charity that can make a religious house what it should be. The smaller the community, the greater the necessity for universal charity and all this imports. It is inconceivable that a spirit of individualism prevailed in the Holy Family.

Lastly, I should like to consider the obedience of Christ at Nazareth. In the psalms we read of Christ, "In the head of the Book it is written that I should do your will, O Lord, my God." St. Paul says of Jesus, "He was obedient even to the death of the cross." There are, currently, some very bizarre ideas regarding obedience. One's view of obedience runs the peril of being very subjective. If an obedience pleases or measures up to expectations, then fine; otherwise, it is considered subject to debate.

I hardly think that we would find this type of dialogue in

Nazareth. Remember what I said a moment ago. He who spun the firmament into existence, who knows the number of stars, and who is wisdom himself submits himself to the authority of Mary and Joseph. Christ could have called on his divine knowledge and made a better chair or table than could Joseph; or he could have called upon his divine knowledge to teach Joseph, and yet he permits himself to be told "You do not do it that way, Jesus." Christ did not say, "Who says you do not? It's *my* way or no way."

It is unquestionable that some superiors have abused and still do abuse their authority in the exercise of obedience. Were a superior to assert that she was certain of the mind of God in a particular instance, it would be tantamount to claiming a private revelation. How does the superior know she is giving her subject the opportunity to do the will of God? Because as superior she is *legitimately* exercising her authority. How does the subject know she is being given the opportunity to do the will of God? Because the subject has agreed to accept the Rule and the authority of her superior, it is the will of God that she obey her superior's legitimate directives. The subject does it, not because the superior's judgment necessarily corresponds with the mind of God, but because she has vowed to accept as the will of God in her regard the things that the superior has lawfully told her to do.

An excessive concern over obedience is evident today. There is a fear that one's personality is going to be warped if she does not assert herself and if she does not actually see the superior's command as the most reasonable thing to do. This is a genuine mistake. Obedience is one virtue or vow the practice of which does not become easier as we advance in age. Obedience, properly understood, is the most perfect of all human virtues under charity, because we yield that to God which is most noble in ourselves, our intellect and will.

10 *Baptism of Our Lord*

Then Jesus came from Galilee to John, at the Jordan, to be baptized by him. And John was for hindering him, and said, "It is I who ought to be baptized by thee, and dost thou come to me?" But Jesus answered and said to him, "Let it be so now, for so it becomes us to fulfill all justice." Then he permitted him. And when Jesus had been baptized, he immediately came up from the water. And behold, the heavens were opened to him, and he saw the Spirit of God descending as a dove and coming upon him. And behold, a voice from the heavens said, "This is my beloved Son, in whom I am well pleased." (Matt. 3:13–17.)

Fr. Christoph: In this quotation Christ identifies himself with sinful man by taking his place alongside sinful man. Early heresies either denied the humanity or the divinity of Christ. Yet, if there is anything that the Second Person of the Holy Trinity insisted upon, it was that he was fully a member of the human race; he gloried in the title "Son of Man."

Fr. Evoy: Our Lord is like unto us in all things, sin excepted. He is fully a member of the human race. As such he is the exemplar for *all* of us in all that is properly human. His behavior was the wisest, the most prudent, the most noble, and yet always so very human. At the same time there are some things he did which we find difficult to understand.

A case in point is found in the Scriptural verses just read. Christ had but thirty-three short years to redeem the human race, and to our natural bewilderment we find him spending about thirty of those years in one unimportant little town. We do not naturally understand why he did not go to such cosmopolitan centers as Alexandria, Athens, and Rome. This episode serves also to bring out the consoling fact that Christ knows from experience what it means to become wholesomely attached to a place. He knows the feeling of sinking roots in a place regarded as home. Moreover, he knows the experience of having, in a sense, to pull up one's roots and move on.

There is something else in this context which would naturally pique our curiosity. How much did he tell his mother about what was going to transpire in the next three years? It is sometimes difficult in our lives to know just how much to tell those we love. The problem lies in determining how much they should be told, even though it would be painful, and how much that is told would constitute unnecessary pain. Did he tell his mother that he had but three years to live? Did he tell her he would be put to death? Crucified? I would imagine he would have told her at least that he would no longer make Nazareth his home. He could not leave her with the hope, never to be attained, that he would return. We can be sure that whatever he told his mother, he did so out of full consideration for her. This considerateness for others which our Lord is exemplifying is one on which we need frequently to reflect and apply to our lives.

Take the matter of our friendships. It is possible to make our own needs the pattern of our relating to other persons. For instance, not only do you have no right whatever to the special friendship of another sister, but real womanly consideration would incline you to be most sensitive to her true needs and most respectful of her feelings in this matter.

Again, we wonder why Christ insisted upon being baptized, since the Baptist's own inclination was clearly opposed to it. In fact, John gave our Lord a good reason why he should not perform the rite. He said openly that he was unworthy. And Christ replied, in effect, "I know that you are not worthy. Now do it because I want you to."

I think that Father Christoph and I, as priests, are particularly conscious of the lesson our Lord is teaching here. It would be the sheerest absurdity for either of us to maintain seriously that he is worthy to administer any sacrament, let alone offer the Sacrifice of the Mass. But Christ did not invite us to share in his priesthood because of our worthiness. Neither has he invited you to lead the religious life because you are worthy. When he was dealing with John the Baptist, our Lord's attitude toward a person's worthiness was unmistakable. He did not disagree that John was unworthy of his vocation, but he added immediately "Suffer it to be so." He then insisted that John baptize him.

We do not need to feel worthy of our vocation, nor inclined to every single thing given us under obedience. Underlying whatever painful experience that may be ours in the course of our lives is a deep gratitude to God for the tremendous vocation that is ours, despite our being undeserving of that vocation.

Note that John "permitted" the will of Christ to prevail over his natural reluctance to perform the baptismal rite. That word *permitted* says so much. It says that John was very far from feeling worthy, let alone enthusiastic, about what our Lord wanted him to do. Christ does not seem to mind the way John felt. Note that our Lord does not demand that John deny or even change his feelings. He instructed John, despite his feelings, to proceed with the baptism.

Sisters, you do not live in community life very long before discovering that under obedience and the demands of common life, you are expected to do some things towards which you are naturally disinclined. There may be times when in the face of a difficult directive, a sister can do little to change her negative feelings. Then, for God, she heroically obeys despite them.

Fr. Christoph: Earlier we reminded you that God chooses to save men through men. This gives us a clue to the reason we have been chosen. And it is rather humbling to reflect on the choice he has made, for God chooses to save men through inept instruments. To prove this we have only to reflect upon our own limitations.

We have remarked that perhaps each one of us knows any number of individuals who, humanly speaking, might be better instruments in the hands of God than we are. And yet God chooses you and he chooses me. I said that this is a humbling thought, but it is also a very comforting one. It is humbling because, in a certain sense, God leans apparently upon the weak for help and support. It is nonetheless a very reassuring reflection. Weak man becomes vital to God's mission. You are vital to his work whether you are a novice, a junior, a sister out in the active apostolate or one along in years who can contribute to his work only by loving. Almighty God knows the beginning, the middle, and the end of your service to him.

As we read in Scripture, he chooses to use weak instruments to confound the strong. Indeed, the simple, the weak, and the ignorant have often been used by Almighty God to carry his message, not because there is any special value in being simple or weak or ignorant, but because God wants to make it very evident that he is the one who is working through human instruments and that man, of himself, can do nothing of supernatural value. This prevents man from becoming proud and from feeling that he, by reason of his individual gifts, is indispensable to Christ's mission. So it is that Christ proposes to John that John baptize him. The perfect man, without any sin whatever, proposes to

John that a sacramental be given him, thus publicly indicating his identification with sinful man.

Fr. Evoy: The baptism John administered was not a sacrament, as Father Christoph just mentioned, but a sacramental. It was not a sacrament because it did not bestow a participation in divine life. It was rather a sign of one's renunciation of sin. Why did Christ choose to go through a ceremony renouncing his nonexistent sins? Are we not being taught here that every apostolic undertaking should begin with the renunciation of sin? Christ was really saying, by submitting to this baptism, "As I here among men begin the public phase of my Father's business with the renunciation of sin, I give you an example that you should also begin each undertaking of your Father's business with the renunciation of sin." His Father himself put his seal on this beginning when he said, "This is my beloved Son in whom I am well pleased. Hear you him."

There is another thought here. The baptism administered by John had something in common with the sacrament of baptism. Both symbolize a dying to sin and to inordinate love of self. In fact, St. Paul tells us that we are baptized into death and through death into life.

Fr. Christoph: In the one who is going to carry on the work of Christ within the religious vocation there must be a new dedication and express renunciation not only of sin but of everything in the past which is unsuited to religious life. This is why in some religious communities the investiture ceremony begins with a cloth being thrown over the postulant, covering her completely. Afterwards the novice is clothed in a habit. She may even be given a new name to signify her commitment to a new way of life. She is still the same person. She has the same nature, the same likes and dislikes. But the Church uses this symbolism to emphasize the severing of herself from her past way of life and her new identification with Christ.

Until the time of the ceremony marking the beginning of his Public Life, Jesus was identified by his fellowmen with the community in which he lived. At the Jordan his Father makes it unmistakably clear to all that Christ belongs to the whole world. Christ's public ministry is about to commence, and he prepared himself for it by an act which unmistakably manifests his identification with all humanity.

Fr. Evoy: I think we would do well to look further into the symbolic aspect of the religious garb about which Father Christoph was speaking. In many communities the postulant wears a black veil symbolizing death. The death symbolized here is not to her own person but only to that which is inordinate in her behavior, to that in her which impedes the living of her complete commitment to God. By no means does it signify a dying to the nature God has given her. There has been some confusion in religious life about this matter of dying to self. God made each sister the person she is. He created her as *this* unique person. Her individuality is a sacred heritage that she must safeguard. At the same time, there are in her inordinate tendencies which tend to be unruly and get into the way of her *for-God-ness*. And it is precisely to these tendencies that she endeavors to die.

When St. Paul points out our need to die to the old man, he is not saying that we should die to the man, but to the *old* man in us. We ought never die to our true self. We should never attempt to eliminate those things which are proper to us as individuals. Indeed, each one ought not only to retain but to develop her own distinctive individuality.

The novice wears a white veil. White symbolizes the purified life of a religious at her best, living joyfully as the unique person she is. Whiteness symbolizes also dedication in religious life.

She strives to serve God generously with the talents he has given her. In this way she tends to avoid the tragic error of those who have endeavored to divest themselves of their own individuality and have thus changed themselves into largely depersonalized religious-garbed caricatures of women.

The knowledge that she is living the religious dedication symbolized by the white veil becomes the key to her joyfulness. And religious life should be joyful. I am not implying that one should go about at all times with a big smile on her face, but rather that she should not be wearing a look of discontent, and truth to tell, some do just that.

On profession day the novice receives the black veil. This symbolizes that she must henceforth live calmly vigilant, lest the inclinations leading to death slip back undetected into her life.

Fr. Christoph: It is a kind of truism that you tend to be as professed religious what you were before you entered. And this, in a sense, is what you should be. Common life is nurtured by the observance of your rules and constitutions, your customs and common activities, but it should never be achieved at the cost of surrendering your individuality. I would like to repeat what Father Evoy said a moment ago. In the past there has been too much emphasis in communtiy life on uniformity. You entered the novitiate and took your place in the long line. At the end of that period of probation you emerged with the same physical characteristics still distinctive. But often enough your pattern of thinking, speaking, your mannerisms, your initiative, your imaginativeness, your uniqueness have not survived with comparable integrity.

You are all to be imitators of Christ, but in your own unique way. You are all to bring Christ to your neighbors, but hopefully as this particular real woman. Your following of Christ must be *your* following of Christ in which your uniqueness must find expression. Hence your following of Christ must find manifesta-

tion through the employment of your talents within the framework of your temperament and personality—that which is so
distinctive of you. It should be left to your own initiative and
responsibility to bring out this wholesome individuality. In this
way, religious are best able to bring a wealth and variety of
talents into play in a community.

Fr. Evoy: I think all of you would be horrified if you ever heard
of an organization which required that all its members undergo
radical cosmetic surgery in order that every one would look exactly like every other one. Even on the assumption that the final
physical appearance would be a highly presentable one, you
would still be shocked. Your position would be that if God
wanted these persons to look alike, he would have made them
alike.

Now if God had wanted all of you to operate alike psychologically, he would have made you all carbon copies of an original. But he did not. The parallel is clear. It would be just as
erroneous to think that in religious life you have to be molded,
shaped, and formed all alike in every detail of behavior. God
made all of you human beings, yet he did not design any one of
you to act exactly like any other. To blot out all that is distinctive of each of you would be to destroy God's creation.

Moreover, God loves each of you as the unique person he
created, and not just as one of the sisters. And God wants you to
love him as *you* are and to be the real woman he wants you to
be. You simply are not that someone else, and so you cannot
love him as that someone else does. Your love of God should
always come from the love of the real person that you are here
and now. Accordingly, it would be a real fallacy if ever your
love for him were to become the "if only" kind—"If only I had
more education"—"If only I had been a more generous religious"
—"if only"—"if only. . . ." The "if only" approach to your love

of God is tragic. There are thousands of "if onlys" which could be used to keep you from giving yourself, in love, to God.

I recall the intriguing book title *From Where the Sun Now Stands*. It is from where you now stand that God wants you to give him a service that is the manifestation of your love. There is another consideration here. There might be a place on this earth from which God has never been loved. That place might well be a classroom or a hospital corridor. And while it is impossible for you to be certain that your love is the first he has ever received from that place, you can be certain that no one else ever has loved him from that spot just exactly as you love him. No one else could possibly give him your personal love.

Now it becomes increasingly clear why you have a sacred God-given duty to protect the entirety of that which is most properly you—the unique you God made from love. Indeed, you are not morally free to disregard this obligation to safeguard the *you* he created. You do not have absolute ownership over yourself. Accordingly you may not destroy any part of the real you but only employ yourself according to the will of your owner. This is a matter of justice. You simply do not have the right to exercise absolute dominion by destroying any part of you. Even religious life does not constitute an exception to this. You are not permitted the unauthorized destruction of anything which is properly you. Though you live under religious obedience, you still retain the stewardship over yourself for which you must some day render an account.

Fr. Christoph: Upon entering religious life you are helped by those who have experience and who are delegated to teach you the principles of religious life, to help you correct those aspects of your behavior not suited to religious life. It is never the role of religious superiors to try to uproot or destroy what God has given you and what makes you uniquely you and must be found in you as a real woman.

It is true that sometimes the talent, for instance, God has given you may not seem of very much value in religious life. There may be little or no opportunity to exercise it. Ballet dancing might be a case in point. There is, I imagine, little call for ballet dancing in a religious community. If you have this talent, it is almost certain that it is going to be, in the main, a hidden talent. However, this is but one expression of your uniqueness which surely can find other channels of expression. After all, your uniqueness is not exhausted solely in this one talent. My point is that you should not necessarily equate any past pattern of behavior with the *real* you.

Fr. Evoy: You are going to express the real you in many ways. You did not leave your talents outside the door when you entered religious life. Quite the contrary. You should seek to find expression for every talent you have within the framework of your religious life.

I feel that many religious who have been very effective in their apostolic life have used a great many talents. In fact, I have often wondered if some of them did not, on occasion, effectively use talents of dubious worth.

In this context, I recall Father Daniel Lord, of whom most of you have at least heard. Near the end of his life I heard him sing publicly for a group of people to his own piano accompaniment. At that time, in my judgment, he no longer possessed a singing voice of solo caliber. But as I recall it, that fact, which I noted at once, did not bother me in the least. I was preoccupied with the fascinating personality coming through that mediocre voice. He was Father Daniel Lord all the way—with the spotlight on Christ. And if he had not been Father Daniel Lord from the top of his head down to his toes, he could not have presented our Lord that way.

It is so important to remind yourself that the Christ you present to others is always Christ as you personally know and

love him—your Christ. He comes through to others as your
Christ, not the community's Christ. This remains true even
though your presentation of him will always be within the
framework of the activities proper to your community. You
radiate Christ to people from the depths of your own person. It
would, therefore, be unreal for me to try to put forth Christ as
he is known and loved by Father Christoph.

Fr. Christoph: There is a tendency in us to imitate and to
identify with those whom we love. If there were a slavish imitation, an effort to ape what seems to be uniquely the personality
of another, it would be unbecoming because in the process we
would lose that which makes us unique. St. Paul could write to
his Corinthian converts, "Be you imitators of me as I am of
Christ." He showed them how they were to imitate Christ. St.
Paul made the virtues of Christ his own by fitting them into his
own personality.

The example of the heroes of Christ are presented to us for our
admiration and even for our imitation. The patience, the love,
the generosity of this or that model are held up to us, but each
is to manifest this patience, this love, or generosity in a way
appropriate to his own personality. We are to be ourselves. The
Incarnate Son of God acted in a manner becoming himself. We
are accordingly to be Christlike without ever ceasing to be ourselves. Nor does the triumphant remark of St. Paul "I live now
not I but Christ lives in me" deny this position.

St. Paul remained true to his real self throughout his life. St.
Peter was St. Paul's companion in Rome. Both were most Christlike, yet the personalities and characters of these two were very
different. Here we have the example of two men, very close to
God, whose apostolic careers resembled each other's so much, yet
whose Christlike behavior was invariably an expression of their
own personalities.

Another observation on this episode suggests itself here. It is interesting to find that the Eternal Father was able to look down upon his Son whose life up to this point was quite unspectacular, whose work was equally ordinary, and whose role in the history of the world up to this time was apparently insignificant, and say of him, "This is my beloved Son in whom I am well pleased."

What we have told you some time ago about achieving sanctity through the performance of ordinary tasks bear repetition here. For it is not fame, public recognition, or any other such attainment that makes you pleasing to God. It is doing the ordinary things for the love of God. The opportunity to do the extraordinary seldom, if at all, comes into the lives of most men and women. It seems that God himself is willing to be satisfied with a life characterized by ordinariness. If you want God to be able to say of you, "This is my beloved in whom I am well pleased," the reason most likely for his approval will be not so much what you do as the manner in which you do it, that is, with real love and devotion.

Fr. Evoy: In this New Testament scene of Christ's baptism, John teaches us a great deal. Later on our Lord was to praise John publicly for his courage. John did show tremendous courage. It took courage for him to confront Herod with the fact that he was living in adultery with his brother's wife, Herodias. It took courage to tell the Scribes and Pharisees to their faces that they were hypocrites and a brood of vipers. Note that Christ praised John for his courage, not for his fearlessness. If John had been fearless he could not be an example of courage to us. He was not fearless. He was afraid. Indeed, had he not been afraid he could not have shown courage. We must remind ourselves that unless a person is afraid, there is no such thing as courage. Now love, as our ultimate motivation, in no way rules out courage, precisely because love does not blot out all fear. We can show our love through courage while yet afraid. And there are times when this is called for. Indeed, there are occasions when such courage demands the heroic.

11 *The Temptation of Our Lord*

Then Jesus was led into the desert by the Spirit, to be tempted by the devil. And after fasting forty days and forty nights, he was hungry. And the tempter came and said to him, "If thou art the Son of God, command that these stones become loaves of bread." But he answered and said, "It is written, *Not by bread alone does man live, but by every word that comes forth from the mouth of God.*"

Then the devil took him into the holy city and set him on the pinnacle of the temple, and said to him, "If thou art the Son of God, throw thyself down; for it is written, *He will give his angels charge concerning thee; and upon their hands they shall bear thee up, lest thou dash thy foot against a stone.*" Jesus said to him, "It is written further, *Thou shalt not tempt the Lord thy God.*"

Again, the devil took him to a very high mountain and showed him all the kingdoms of the world and the glory of them. And he said to him, "All these things will I give thee, if thou wilt fall down and worship me." Then Jesus said to him, "Begone, Satan! for it is written, *The Lord thy God shalt thou worship and him only shalt thou serve.*"

Then the devil left him; and behold, angels came and ministered to him. (Matt. 4:1–11.)

Fr. Christoph: Unless there is evidence to the contrary, it is a reasonable assumption that we were moved by excellent motives to enter religious life. We continue in this life, hopefully guided by the Holy Spirit in the pursuit of our own perfection and the salvation of others according to the rules and constitutions of our community. Throughout our religious life there are occasions when we have to make important decisions, some of which may drastically affect our life, especially our spiritual life.

The occasion of Christ being tempted brings to the fore the need for a highly developed ability to discern spirits. It is not always clear what we should do. The subtle influence of our baser passions, our inordinate attachments, or the devil himself, and not the love and service of God, may be responsible for our decisions. In all the determinations that you are free to make, you want to be guided by the Holy Spirit. You must realize that there are factors within and outside of you opposed to the movements of the Holy Spirit in you. These forces could stand in the way of your closer union with God. You should be able to discern what things are temptations, what things are not, and how to deal with temptations. Most of all, you should realize that temptations are not evidences of your unworthiness.

Holy Scripture says "Son, when thou entereth into the service of the Lord, prepare thyself for temptations." Again, "the just man is tried by temptations." In order that we might recognize and know how to deal with temptations, Christ who is like us in all things, sin alone excepted, permits himself to be exposed to temptations. True, he could not be tempted in the same way that we are tempted, because temptation is an inducement to do evil. Obviously evil could never in any guise be attractive to Jesus Christ, the God-man. But the same external things that would be a temptation to the average person were presented to Christ in Satan's futile hope that Christ would be moved by them.

You should not think that temptation always comes from the devil. Temptation may also originate from yourself. Even in religious life you may be strongly tempted by your own natural inclinations. Moreover, temptation can be very alluring. The more serious temptations are normally not presented as serious. The evil spirit knows our commitment and our tendency to flee mortal sin. So for the most part you are tempted to lesser sins and if you succumb, then you are tempted to those which are more seriously sinful. I think one lesson that our Lord is teaching here is that we are not to compromise with temptation. Another lesson is that the devil characteristically searches for each person's Achilles heel. Each of us has real weaknesses and these the devil seeks to discover. If he does not know them, he will continue to look for them.

Fr. Evoy: In the scene we are contemplating, Satan waits until Christ has been weakened by the long fast. Then he moves in. Satan always fights dirty. He takes every possible advantage. There is not the slightest trace of the gentleman about him. Truth is not in him. He is totally without love, without honor, without honesty, even without pity. No treachery is too base; nothing is beneath him. This is something that takes a long, long time to learn. We continue to be surprised at the cunning of his tactics.

Once he finds our Achilles heel he moves right in. If your weakness is jealousy, he will concentrate on that; if it is impurity, he will strive in that area to destroy you and perhaps another through you. If you do not really love others, he will have a field day in that area. He will find out where you are weakest and then stoop to any means to destroy you. His motivation is consuming hate—hatred of God and God's loved ones. Hatred is second in strength only to love. The devil will gladly pay any price to destroy you. Remember, you are God's. That is all Satan needs for motivation to want to destroy you eternally. He never stops his fight against you, and remember he can be depended upon always to fight dirty.

Fr. Christoph: I think it is important to emphasize what Father Evoy has just said, that hate is second in strength only to love. Just as one who loves will find so many ways to manifest that love, so Satan, from hate, is inventive in discovering our weaknesses and in capitalizing on them. He is so clever and cunning. He is a veteran campaigner with angelic intelligence and therefore able to take almost anyone by surprise. For he knows our weaknesses better than we do. He can be unbelievably subtle.

Invariably he uses something that is attractive, in his efforts to secure his ends. Satan distorts the beautiful and good to bring about our downfall. He knows where we are vulnerable. He knows our love of ease; he knows our sensuality; he knows our egotism and our pride. He knows the attraction of so much in this world. So he takes advantage of these to ensnare us. We have to be knowledgeable about our weaknesses. Part of the purpose of meditating is to uncover and openly acknowledge to ourselves our own peculiar weaknesses. Against these, you must strengthen yourselves by ever deepening your personal love for God and your neighbor.

St. Peter says the devil goes about like a roaring lion seeking whom he may devour. The figure the Apostle uses of a lion seeking whom he may devour very aptly expresses the character of the devil, his viciousness and the catlike behavior with which he operates. A lion patiently stalks his prey. And Satan is patient.

Fr. Evoy: St. Peter's use of the figure of Satan as a lion roaring is very apt. Since we have all been to a zoo and at close range have heard a lion roar, we know how frightening this can be. If frightening a person will serve the devil's purpose, he will do just that. He can roar when it is useful. He will roar at the person who is already afraid if he feels that he can frighten the person more. As women, you know that when a man shouts at you, you cringe. You might shout back, but something inside you wilts. With any one of you the devil's roaring might be effective.

Keep in mind that he fights dirty. The only thing you can depend upon is that he will use every conceivable weapon against you. He is the master liar. You can believe nothing he tells you. Notice the lies in the Scriptural account of his tempting Christ. "All of these things will I give you," he says to our Lord. Lies! He owns none of them.

In view of the foregoing remarks your consideration of the devil ought to begin with a calm confrontation of the facts. You are dealing with a most capable, loathsome adversary who has determined to do everything possible to destroy you. But powerful as this fallen angel is, he is limited by God in what he can do. Within this framework of what he can do, he will use every deceit and every cunning, some of which you may not have recognized as such. Remember, you are dealing with a highly intelligent, wholly dishonest being.

Fr. Christoph: A point to reflect upon is why God permits the devil to do these things. For the past few decades some non-Catholic theologians have relegated the devil to mythology. Nevertheless, they said that he has played a role in human history, for the myth itself has been an effective deterrent of immoral behavior. There is a reassessment of this attitude today, and, indeed, there is currently a growing acceptance among non-Catholic theologians that diabolical forces are at work in the world.

A Christian may have some difficulty in reconciling with God's mercy, goodness, and providence the fact that he permits the devil to tempt man. St. Thomas offers a reasonable solution to this problem. He reminds us, in the first place, that God always acts purposefully. Hence he could not permit a creature to be without a purpose. If the devil did not in some way fit into the plans of Divine Providence, then God, it would seem, would have acted without purpose. How does God then bring the devil within the framework of his all-wise providence? St. Thomas says

that God allows the devil to tempt man and when man over-
comes the devil's solicitations, he becomes more pleasing to God;
so, unwittingly, Satan contributes to man's sanctification.

Father Evoy said that the devil fights dirty. Christ was hungry.
Could you think of a more despicable thing than to deliberately
exploit the need of a man in this type of situation? The devil
tempts Christ by saying that if he is God, he can turn the stones
to bread. It is interesting to notice the limitations of Satan's
knowledge in his hypothetical remark *"if* you are the Son of
God."

Fr. Evoy: Another point to note is that when people deny his
existence, the devil can work more effectively. This is why he is
happy when his existence is explained away. To be explained
away means that he can proceed with his efforts to destroy people
with much less danger of being detected. He can thus fight in-
sidiously with less risk of being discovered. So consumed is he
with the craving to destroy those loved by God that he will gladly
sacrifice the spotlight of recognition to gain his purposes.

We need to remind ourselves repeatedly that he hates with a
black, everlasting hate. And just as love seeks to enrich and
safeguard the one loved, so hate strives to destroy another. Satan
cannot attack our Lord in his personal humanity, but he can
get at him in the persons of his suffering members. Would that
we had such a clear recognition, as has the devil, of the Whole
Christ, Christ's Mystical Body.

Satan proves himself the master of deception in his encounters
with us. Seldom does he present us with temptations which
appear to be clear-cut violations either of ourselves or of another
person. The temptations he employs are usually presented as
having some grounds or some "reasons" in their favor.

For example, look at the temptation he presented to Christ,
"All these things will I give thee, if thou wilt bow down and
adore me." He avoids here any naked statement that things are

of paramount importance and so persons are to be subordinated to things. Rather, in glowing terms he presents to our Lord the value of "all these things" and then indicates that in order to have them the only thing he has to do is violate his own person by giving to one, other than God, that which belongs only to God. And the devil knew well that he would not even have to point out to Christ that "all these things" could be used for the glory of God.

Satan has had centuries of experience of presenting temptation with real finesse. He can even portray, as a zealous and virtuous act, the sacrificing of another person. Such a sacrifice might be urged for the sake of peace, or for advancement of a great work, or for some other worthwhile purpose. The devil can present himself, as Scripture reminds us, as the father of light. Strange that the father of lies should be able to pass himself off as the father of light. But he is exceedingly adept in the use of sophistry. He can tell us that our motives are justifiable, while we are actually sinning against charity in ways that are almost incredible.

By way of example, I, as Sister Superior, feel obliged to help Sister Christoph, my religious subject, mend her ways. Sister has openly failed to conform to regulations in the community. So, I have no doubt that I am acting from high motivation when I determine to correct Sister, by refusing to talk to her for several days.

Do you think for a moment I could be seriously tempted really to hurt Sister by treating her with complete coldness for any lesser reason? Never. That would be unthinkable. I get tricked into doing it because I fail to recognize this for the lie that it is. I erroneously assume that I have an obligation to correct her by my prolonged silence, precisely because I really care about her and because I am zealous for the proper discipline of the community. And Satan is delighted. As long as I do not see that I am doing something really destructive to Sister, the devil is satisfied. And most probably I can be persuaded to repeat this hurtful pattern in the future with Sister or with others. And nothing, in what I am doing, strikes me as actually damaging to this person. Meanwhile, the devil is satisfied with what I am doing.

Fr. Christoph: "I am going to teach her a needed lesson. After all, for the sake of the community, somebody has to put her in her place." Correcting Sister could be most legitimate under certain circumstances, but this manner of correcting is one in which a serious violation of charity could masquerade as virtue. The expectation is that everyone is going to be tempted along the lines which accord with her own personal characteristics. Hence one may fail to recognize them as temptations, and a vice bears the mark of a virtue. The devil has made progress here.

Sisters, there are temptations so unbecoming that some good religious cannot admit even experiencing them. They are felt to be so out of keeping with religious vocation! These are temptations principally involving chastity.

St. Thomas tells us that there is one temptation the devil takes particular delight in suggesting. This is the temptation to impurity. The devil has no body; hence he was never in a position to commit sins of the flesh. To see someone use his body in such a way as to defeat the purposes for which God created it gives the devil a unique satisfaction, just as one's refusal to succumb to temptations of this nature produces in the devil a unique kind of hatred. Greatness in an individual can be manifested in overcoming these temptations which in a real sense are according to human nature.

Sometimes among religious women a strong temptation against the vow of chastity is regarded as a sin. Such a temptation might also be incorrectly viewed as evident proof of God's displeasure, or one's intrinsic unworthiness, and hence a sign that one does not belong in religious life. A religious might believe that no dedicated person could ever have thoughts like these.

Fr. Evoy: Perhaps it would never occur to a sister that being troubled by the flesh is evidence that she is human. While the sexual urge might remain dormant in a woman for a lengthy period of time, were she never to have such a feeling, it could be matter for concern. Whenever in her feelings for another person a woman becomes aware of the emergence of the physical, she calmly copes with it. A sister ought not to find this urgency to the physical so persistently strong that it demands almost continuous heroic control on her part. But were a sister never to have experienced some problems, it would be unusual.

The sacrifice of a sister under the vow of chastity entails the renunciation of the love of a husband, of motherhood and of a home of her own.

If a sister has never found the observance of chastity personally costly, it might well be asked how meaningful was her renunciation under this vow.

It is of some moment to reflect here that were a sister to deliberately entertain that which was in any way opposed to her vow of chastity, it would actually be a form of stealing. Hence, were she to yield to what was clearly opposed to her vow, after having given herself *completely* to God, she would be taking back what she had surrendered to him. She did not *have* to take the vow of chastity. Presumably, as a completely free agent, she offered it. This "taking back" reminds us of the account in the Acts about the behavior of Ananias and Sapphira. They said that they had turned in all their earthly wealth. They did not have to do this. The commitment was a free act. But secretly they had held back a little something for themselves.

Their wrong was similar in this regard to the wrong in a religious who vows chastity to God and then deliberately and secretly keeps for herself part of what she has given up under her vow of chastity. I am also concerned with the sister who, even though she may not clearly recognize it, has actually held back for herself some area which she vowed to give over to God under chastity. This reservation could be the hidden source of many of her failings in the matter of her vow.

Fr. Christoph: One of the prepotent drives in human beings is the sexual instinct. It is important to be aware of its strength. Father Evoy said if a religious woman has never experienced this kind of temptation it is rather extraordinary, because this drive is rooted in human nature.

It would be unhealthy for her to deny to herself that she had experienced temptations against purity. Her persistent denial would prevent her from facing an unpleasant reality. As a consequence, she would not strengthen herself for the onslaught of the devil. This pattern of denial in a religious could have the result that after ten, fifteen, or twenty years in religious life she could suddenly be confronted with a temptation against purity in which she would be overcome. It would take her by surprise because for so long a time she had told herself that even a temptation against purity was unthinkable.

Fr. Evoy: We need to be even more specific here with respect to the content of these temptations. To the extent that you are a genuine woman, any time you really come to know a good person, you are going to love him with the love of neighbor. Clearly, your love admits of many degrees. And of course, it is quite possible for you to love a good person without finding that individual personally attractive. You might admire, respect, and like a person and not be strongly attracted to that person. Most of you do not have a great deal of contact with men. You might however find yourself, possibly to your surprise, feeling a personal attraction toward your pastor, dentist, doctor, janitor, or some other man. Should such be the case, if you are not wholly a real woman, it might be more difficult for you to exercise control over the physical expression of your inclination.

Father Christoph has indicated that any denial of the reality of such a feeling would be unwholesome. You begin to deal with any such temptation by honestly confronting it, rather than by denying its presence in you. Avoiding recourse to the panic button, you proceed as calmly as possible to take whatever measures appear most suitable to maintain proper control. Right here, however, lurks the danger of self-deception for you if you are not a real woman. You could fall prey to the error of coping with such attraction to a man by telling yourself that your love for this person is purely spiritual. Sisters, I am afraid I do not understand what this kind of purely spiritual love is. If your love is real, then you love someone as you are, and you are a woman. Your personal love for another, therefore, must be that of a genuine woman.

Fr. Christoph: We call this kind of purely spiritual love platonic love, and truly it belongs exclusively in Plato's cave. It surely does not exist anywhere else. We are human beings. We tend to be drawn to an attractive person when we meet such a person. This is natural. Yet, we should be fully aware that in any given attraction there could be some danger. Our first line of defense against such temptation is the calm recognition of the possibility of such danger. We know that there are certain expressions of love which we may manifest becomingly to those of our own sex as well as to those of the opposite sex. We ought also to be able to recognize what is improper in this regard.

Fr. Evoy: In fact, I think it is well to acknowledge to yourselves that some of you are capable of playing a game in this area of relating personally to another person. Some of you have it in you to be coy and even flirtatious. And at the very same time you are capable of denying to yourself that you are doing either of these. Playing such a game need not be morally wrong. But it would be unbecoming for you to do so. You would expect to see such behavior in an immature girl or a female of dubious virtue rather than in a woman. Should you, on occasion, find yourself playing any such game, to deny you were doing so would be dishonest. Moreover, to refuse your experience admission into your awareness is unhealthy.

Coping with any inclination towards unacceptable behavior becomes effective only after it is faced. You ought not deny the existence of any part of your experience. It is rather a matter of acknowledging all of your experience and then striving intelligently and consistently to control whatever tends to be out of bounds.

When you find that you are personally attracted to someone, you face that fact fully. It would be most unrealistic to expect that you would never again find someone personally attractive simply because you have donned a religious habit. While it would be unthinkable that a real woman would be sexually attracted to every personally attractive individual, she still makes some sacrifices under her vow. Rather than concluding that you would have to make no further sacrifices to God under your vow of chastity, quite the opposite would be expected. Such sacrifices you should be prepared to make perhaps every week of your life.

Fr. Christoph: I do not know why Father said "every week of your life." It is every day of your life. What makes your dedication and your holocaust to God of such great value is that each day you renew your entire commitment, including, therefore, your vow of chastity. Because you are social by nature you are constantly coming into contact with other people. You should not be surprised if at times you are tempted even strongly against purity. It is not often that poverty causes any deep concern. The opportunities to violate this vow are relatively limited. In addition, the temptations to go counter to the expressed commands of superiors are comparatively infrequent. But there are many opportunities in which you have to exercise control over your affections in order to avoid serious sin.

It is unfortunate that this matter of impurity is not discussed as it should be in religious conferences. Hence it is easy enough for one to feel that she is unique in having such an experience. And since such a sin may be felt to be unthinkable in a religious, it is readily understood how one could feel that it is something which is very difficult to confess.

Temptations are going to last at least as long as one fights with them. The more one concentrates on fighting temptations, the more one calls attention to them. Prayer at the time of temptation may not be the answer to the question of how best to deal with it, because as long as one prays she may keep the temptation in her imagination. St. Thomas suggests distractive activity as a practical help. However, no one can gainsay the value for the same end of the practice of the Presence of God.

Fr. Evoy: The fact that a temptation against chastity remains obstinately present would mean normally that it is being deliberately entertained. Such a temptation ordinarily will not continue to thwart a sister's best efforts to drive it away. If she has indulged the temptation for some time, it may not be possible to turn the focus of her attention away from the temptation and to concentrate on something else. She could indeed, as Father Christoph indicated, use the pretext of praying about this temptation, asking God to take it from her, while doing nothing about it herself, as a justification for further focusing her attention on it.

Fr. Christoph: Let me remind you of the Scriptural quotation, "The just man is tried by temptation." Hence temptation is the lot of everyone, especially of you who are striving for sanctity. What you do about your temptations contributes much to whether you will be a saint or a sinner. In the rules for the Discernment of Spirits you are reminded by St. Ignatius that you should be steadfast in your behavior especially in a period of emotional turbulence. You are warned not to act in haste nor to make a decision under the stress of emotion. Indeed, you might live to regret such a decision. You should develop a healthy attitude towards temptation, confident, according to the words of St. Paul, that God "will with temptation make issue that you need never fall." You, by yourselves, without God's grace would be no match, as we have seen, for the wiles of the devil, but "if Christ is with us who then can be against us." These comforting words, again from St. Paul, should inspire you with confidence, but never to the point of presumption.

12 *Wedding at Cana*

And on the third day a marriage took place at Cana of Galilee, and the mother of Jesus was there. Now Jesus too was invited to the marriage, and also his disciples. And the wine having run short, the mother of Jesus said to him, "They have no wine." And Jesus said to her, "What wouldst thou have me do, woman? My hour has not yet come." His mother said to the attendants, "Do whatever he tells you."

Now six stone water-jars were placed there, after the Jewish manner of purification, each holding two or three measures. Jesus said to them, "Fill the jars with water." And they filled them to the brim. And Jesus said to them, "Draw out now, and take to the chief steward." And they took it to him.

Now when the chief steward had tasted the water after it had become wine, not knowing whence it was (though the attendants who had drawn the water knew), the chief steward called the bridegroom, and said to him, "Every man at first sets forth the good wine, and when they have drunk freely, then that which is poorer. But thou hast kept the good wine until now."

This first of his signs Jesus worked at Cana of Galilee;

and he manifested his glory, and his disciples believed in him. After this he went down to Capharnaum, he and his mother, and his brethren, and his disciples. And they stayed there but a few days. (John 2:1–12.)

Fr. Evoy: It might seem strange to us that our Lord, knowing that he had only three years remaining for his public ministry, would have taken the time to attend this celebration. If his presence at the Cana ceremony had been solely a matter of giving appropriate recognition to the dignity of the institution of marriage, we would readily understand. To bestow such a tribute, it would have sufficed had Christ been present for the marriage ceremony itself. Yet he was unquestionably present at the marriage *feast* as well. St. Matthew narrates that his disciples also were guests at the wedding celebration. In fact, we might somewhat facetiously inquire whether the presence of these same disciples had anything to do with the lamentable fact that the supply of wine had run out. At any rate, as we contemplate the scene at Cana we ought to note that what is rightly important to his friends is important also to Christ.

Mary, as we indicated earlier, showed herself very much the real woman at Cana. I suspect that the men present would have noticed the problem just as soon as there was no further replenishment of the wine. It is doubtful if any of them would have noticed it before that. But a real woman would notice it. Mary noticed it immediately. As a real woman she was very conscious of a social situation, especially one that contained social embarrassment and hurt to those for whom she cared. Notice that there was nothing in her of the "busybody," nothing of going about nosing into this and that. Far from it. She showed the badge of the truly concerned, truly caring woman.

She looked about, not with an eye to find fault but rather with one to protect from pain and hurt. While the "busybody" invariably looks for what is wrong, the real woman looks for what could cause hurt to others so that she might ward off that hurt. A woman's highly sensitive and delicate perceptiveness can be employed by her either to benefit or hurt others.

Our Lady noticed that something was wrong at Cana because she sensed the embarrassment of her hosts. Immediately, as a real woman, she made it her business to find out the source of that embarrassment. Once she had discovered that the lack of wine was the cause, why did she not simply accept it and let it go at that?

That is a reaction some men might expect in a woman. A man could reason, "After all, what could she do about it?" Mary certainly had not come with an extra supply of wine. It was highly unlikely that she would have possessed both the finances and means of transportation needed to replenish the supply of wine. In view of these facts a man might wonder why she could not have said, "This is not my problem. I am a guest here. Why should I even concern myself with it?" I think the answer to these questions are all to be found in the fact that Mary was in every sense a real woman.

Now a man could readily size up this same situation and tell himself that it was unfortunate indeed that the wine had run out, but such was the case and so they ought to accept the situation and make the best of it. He could just shrug it off. But he would not even suspect the indescribable mortification that could be here for the bride on her wedding day. I would suspect that the bridegroom would have been embarrassed momentarily at the ribbing from his friends because he had run out of refreshments, but presumably he would be able to take this comparatively small embarrassment right in stride. A woman would know at once that such would not be true for the bride who might recall this humiliation for years. Mary, as a real woman, was fully aware of this. True to the best in womanhood, the fact that she did not know what she could do about it did not at all mean that she intended to do nothing about it. The only thing uncertain was precisely what she would do about it.

Mary caught her son's attention and told him, "They have no wine." Straightforwardly, as would a man, our Lord explained that it would be untimely for him to solve this problem by some extraordinary means. As a real woman so often does, Mary listened closely to his words and understood everything he said. She nodded that she had grasped the picture clearly and then added what she, as a woman, knew was needed. She had been looking at yet another aspect of the problem. She went directly over to the servants and told them to carry out whatever instructions her son would give them.

It would be a mistake to conclude from this contemplation that we have to get our Lady to plead with our Lord for us as if he did not really care about us. Nothing could be further from the truth. But typical of a man, Christ at Cana needed to have his attention called by a woman to a socially embarrassing situation. Christ wants to be importuned. Then he shows clearly that he does really care. And Christ the man seems to need to be influenced here by a real woman's viewpoint.

I am baffled why our Lady went to the servants at all. I do not understand how she could have known that her son would ask them to do anything. What I do see is that she knows her son very well. As she anticipated, our Lord did speak to the servants. He told them to fill the jars with water. There was no sleight-of-hand involved here. Christ did not so much as touch the jars himself. He simply told the servants what to do. Our Lord responds to the appeal of his mother by resorting to extraordinary means. In so doing he shows us that if and when the miraculous is needed, he will perform a miracle. Because he is God he can do the miraculous and because he loves his own he has the motivation to do the miraculous when and where it is called for.

That a miracle had been performed at Cana was clear to everyone aware of the humiliating shortage of wine. His disciples were impressed. I find it difficult to feel any enthusiasm about the fact, as Scripture puts it, that "then his disciples believed in him." What is so admirable about believing *after* seeing his miracle? I would be far more impressed if Scripture had recorded that they had believed in him *before* the miracle. I hope that I am not being unfair to the disciples. But I keep reflecting that although we *know* that he performed many miracles, he certainly would not want us to wait until we witnessed a miracle before we would be willing to believe in him. We recall that after his Resurrection he said to "doubting" Thomas, "Because you have seen, Thomas, you have believed. Blessed are they who have not seen and have believed."

I would like to direct your thoughts once more to our Lady at Cana. She showed herself here a real woman, thoughtful, considerate, and eager to spare others pain and humiliation. As a real woman she is your model, your prototype. Here is the greatest woman in all of history.

Reflect for a moment on a point of Catholic dogma. The person who was elevated to the very peak of human greatness was not a man but a woman. She was *this* woman, Mary, the mother of Christ. In Christ there was no elevation of a person. His person was, and is, divine. What was elevated in Christ was his human nature. Thus when he became man, the Second Person of the Blessed Trinity elevated not his *person* which is divine but his own *human nature*. The human person raised highest was a woman. So lofty has been her elevation that she reigns as Queen of Heaven and includes among her subjects the angels of God.

While our Lord is a model for you and for me in so many ways, our Lady is a model especially for you, precisely in as much as you are a woman. As a woman you have her—in every way a real woman—as your proper model. In the person of this woman whom Christ chose to be his own mother, you discover what kind of a woman Christ wants you to be. It is most important for each of you to recall from time to time that unless you are at your best as a real woman, you are not going to be at your best as an effective religious.

13 *Beatitudes*

And seeing the crowds, he went up the mountain. And when he was seated, his disciples came to him. And opening his mouth he taught them, saying,

"Blessed are the poor in spirit, for theirs is the kingdom of heaven.

Blessed are the meek, for they shall possess the earth.

Blessed are they who mourn, for they shall be comforted.

Blessed are they who hunger and thirst for justice, for they shall be satisfied.

Blessed are the merciful, for they shall obtain mercy.

Blessed are the clean of heart, for they shall see God.

Blessed are the peacemakers, for they shall be called children of God.

Blessed are they who suffer persecution for justice' sake, for theirs is the kingdom of heaven.

Blessed are you when men reproach you, and persecute you, and, speaking falsely, say all manner of evil against you, for my sake.

Rejoice and exult, because your reward is great in heaven; for so did they persecute the prophets who were before you." (Matt. 5:1–12.)

Fr. Christoph: The thunder and lightening of Sinai and the chiseled strength of the Commandments stand out in sharp contrast to the serene simplicity and gentle expression of the Beatitudes pronounced by Christ. The orientation of the Commandments is one to inspire fearful obedience because of God's almighty power. The Sermon on the Mount inspires loving obedience because of Christ's love.

It is significant, too, that Matthew writes, "and opening his mouth he taught them." And his hearers listened and took to heart what Christ said. There is not the slightest evidence that there was any resistance to what he had to say. On the contrary, there is real docility on the part of the disciples.

Today a number of persons, among them religious, have cultivated a questioning attitude toward authority, teachers, and subject matter. We encourage independent thinking, which is good. But along with this independent thinking and questioning attitude there is too often a critical approach which suggests not so much an inquiring mind as disputatiousness. There is no conflict whatever between docility of mind and a desire to know and understand, a quest for answers. Much of the current questioning attitude stems from probably unrecognized intellectual pride. There is even an unwillingness, sometimes, to listen with simplicity. The words of Samuel "Speak Lord, for thy servant heareth" should characterize our docility.

Fr. Evoy: Father Christoph just characterized docility as a willingness to listen. Implicitly at least he included also a desire to learn. It appears to be one of the lessons of history that whenever any major universal change takes place in the way a people lives and does things, there is very little evidence of docility. The participants in revolutions are not normally listening to both sides of issues. This reflection is particularly timely today because there is, in this country, a revolution afoot. Actively engaged in it are some people who appear to be notably different from previous generations.

These persons are seriously concerned about being wholly free to be themselves, and to do their own thinking. They find themselves in revolt against much that is part and parcel of the *status quo*. It is difficult to place the members of this group in a definite age bracket. Perhaps it would not be inaccurate to say that they are, for the most part, in their twenties, thirties, and early forties. Some of them are not notably inclined to do a great deal of listening to those outside their own circle. In fact, they tend to question whether those whose thinking predominantly reflects the present order of things really have much worthwhile to say to them.

Meanwhile, in another group are those who want to give these younger persons the benefit of their greater experience, but they often feel that the less experienced are unwilling to listen. The encountering of such unwillingness to listen can be a frustrating and even a threatening experience. The tendency of those who are thus frustrated is either to attack or to withdraw entirely away from these younger persons. In fact, they can simultaneously experience the inclination both to attack and to withdraw, as would be exemplified by a person who publicly would turn his back upon another and walk away.

It is unfortunate that we find in many areas, including religious life, a growing separation into two groups. In the one group are those who challenge the present order of things; in the other are those who staunchly defend it. Both groups are capable of feeling deeply about their differences. The defenders of the way things are want so much to put the others straight, to show them how things should be done. They find, however, that this other group is really not listening and apparently is not going to listen. The members of the challenging group, moreover, want to discover the truth for themselves. They have an abhorrence for what to them is spoon-fed, predigested intellectual food. To them, such procedure looks suspiciously like brain washing. They want to know, for instance, why things must be done in a certain way. Give them the reasons underlying any current practice, and they will weigh them and decide whether it can be justified. They want to do their own evaluating.

Docility is a virtue that presupposes humility on the part of the teacher as well as on that of the learner. Implicit in genuine humility is the recognition that no mere human being has a monopoly on the truth. It says, moreover, that any given way of doing a thing is normally only one of several possible ways of doing it. In addition, it maintains that because a thing has been done in a certain way over a long period of time it is, by reason of that fact, neither appropriate nor inappropriate to the present.

This holds for so many things—from the way in which a room is to be swept to the manner in which one's prayers are to be said. Because a thing has been done in one particular way over the years is no proof that it should continue to be done that way; it is not even a proof that the thing ought to be done at all. Again, the fact that something has been in vogue a long time does not automatically make it unsuitable to today's needs. There is no reason to believe that whiskey is the only thing that can improve with age!

The frank recognition by everyone, especially by the young, that there is very much still to be learned about almost everything takes humility. For some persons, fighting off the temptation to declare that up until the present time nothing really significant has occurred takes humility. True humility disposes a person to docility—to listen with the desire of learning.

For one of the more experienced group, the temptation may be to feel that because a thing has been done a certain way for years there is no good reason for changing it. She might, moreover, feel irked about "all this nonsense" regarding alleged needs peculiar to this day and age. It takes humility for her to be willing to reconsider the matter with an open mind. The temptation for one of the younger religious group may be to reject auto-matically anything that has been around for a long time simply on the score that it could not possibly be suitable to the present. It takes humility for her to examine with an open mind what she considers "long since moldy."

This is also where meekness enters. When a large strong man turns and walks away from the insulting remark of a small deli-cate individual, his behavior is presumed to be that of meekness rather than weakness. Meekness is strength controlled out of con-sideration for another.

Let us apply this to religious life in a hypothetical situation. Sister Christoph is just beginning her teaching. And I, Sister Evoy, have taught successfully for years. In what I regard as my charity, I am most anxious to show Sister Christoph how to be a good teacher and avoid the costly mistakes I made when I was just starting. But Sister Christoph is not listening. She is, I feel certain, passing up the opportunity of a lifetime. And it hurts me. She surely knows that I am an established teacher in the community and also that my word carries a certain amount of weight.

I am in a position where I could make things quite difficult for this Sister Christoph who is obstinately refusing my offer to help her. But meekness dictates that I do not make things hard for her, that I do not use my strength to make it more difficult for her. While I cannot agree with her in her insistence on learning everything the hard way, because I do not think it wise, I respect her right to do it her way. This is true meekness on my part.

Fr. Christoph: We might examine another aspect of meekness by continuing with Father Evoy's example. Father said that the older teacher had to practise the virtue of meekness. The young teacher, in his example, has likewise to be meek. She should refrain from flaunting her abilities and her achievements and from being inconsiderate towards the older sister even when she disagrees. While the older teacher might be overstepping the bounds of her role when she tries to tell her junior exactly how to teach, on the other hand if the younger sister were to show resentment, it might indicate that she was lacking in meekness. Could she not fail to give the older sister credit for excellent motives in her effort to help? Meekness controls the natural tendency of a real woman to show anger when she is crossed or in any way threatened. Meekness is very truly a virtue of the strong.

Fr. Evoy: Has not what Father Christoph just said been borne out by your own experience? Who has more certain answers to the problems of life than some high school seniors or college sophomores? This is why, when you are dealing with such a person, meekness is called for on your part. You *know* well that the only reason she has the answers is that she has not yet really seen the problems. But you also know that she will not readily accept your wiser admonitions and advice, so out of respect for her human dignity, you refrain from imposing your convictions upon her.

By something of a parallel, I think, Father Christoph is indicating that a young religious may somewhat resemble one of these brashly confident persons. She may never appreciate how little she knows until she reaches middle age. There comes to mind the saying "You can't put an old head on young shoulders." It can be very trying for some older religious to have to refrain from telling these younger persons candidly how little they really know. At times it takes true meekness not to advise and perhaps even reprimand those who, to all appearances, are headed in the wrong direction. And when the older religious reflects, she will come to see that her advantage of thirty or forty years of experience over the younger person does not give her the right to tell the other how to run her life or even how to do a particular task.

Fr. Christoph: The rapid changes in so many areas of knowledge, not only in academic life, but also in the spiritual life—the advances in the study of Scripture, the challenging problems faced in modern moral treatises—leave all of us at times without answers. To impose one's views from the Olympian Heights of his vast experience on those with lesser experience is reasonably offensive to the latter. It is not too difficult to take advantage of one's position. "This is right because I say it is" is not a satisfying answer. It is well for younger religious to be mindful that at times certain unsympathetic remarks by older persons will spring from fear. Their security may have been threatened by the younger person's questioning the traditional ways of doing things. They have, unfortunately, identified the old way of doing things as essential to religious life.

Fr. Evoy: As we mentioned, there are two readily identifiable groups of people in the world and particularly in the Church today. And it is hardly surprising that in each of these you have a small extreme element. First, take the younger, questioning group. In their ranks are some few who state flatly not only that the older group fails to understand them but that it lacks the very ability to understand. These highly articulate few make such sweeping statements as "There has been no vitality in the Church for a thousand years." We would like to hope that ten years from now the recall of such words will prove humorous rather than embarrassing to these same persons. Unfortunately, these few vocal extremists are giving the whole questioning younger group a bad press. It is difficult for many people to take them seriously when they make such statements as "The Church has not really come alive until the latter half of the twentieth century." So unfortunately the whole group comes to take on the appearance of rebellious adolescents. Obviously, such expressed attitudes do not tend to elicit a benevolent response from the more conservative.

Fr. Christoph: Individuals in both groups may lack meekness. The impatience shown and the defensive attitudes maintained attest to this. The older display their lack of meekness in their refusal to yield or to allow for intelligent inquiries and conclusions on the part of the young; the younger, because they so cavalierly sweep aside everything that has been said and done in the past. There cannot be dialogue under these circumstances.

Fr. Evoy: We find in each group some inclination toward its own peculiar extreme. The younger group shows some inclination toward a lack of teachability—not enough listening, not enough openness. This may sound strange, even to them, for as a group they are very concerned about openness. But how can people be open to other people without being willing to listen to them?

Among the older group there are those who also lack openness. "What," they ask, "could these youngsters possibly have to say that would be worth listening to?" They will not permit even one of their own group to attempt to present to them the point of view of the "youngsters," so intent are they upon rightly instructing the "youngsters." Meanwhile, are they themselves willing to listen? Are they implying that age gives them a monoply on truth or wisdom? In their zeal, they want to make sure that the "youngsters" conform, for, they argue, these younger persons are not exceptions and accordingly must be fitted into the pattern of religious life.

The younger group fights tenaciously against being rammed into any mold. As Father Christoph mentioned, when our Lord opened his mouth to speak, the disciples opened their ears. A few of this younger group are so insistent on discovering the truth for themselves that one almost wonders if they would listen even to our Lord. One wonders as well whether a few in the older group would listen to our Lord were he to question some of their traditional ways of doing things.

To make this very practical, no religious, young or old, *has* to take the advice given by unauthorized persons. Ordinary courtesy, however, normally calls for a reasonable attention, even to those who are all too ready to hand out advice. Religious do, however, have an obligation to listen to and obey their superiors. Superiors have the right, and at times even the obligation, to point out certain things to their religious subjects. We are taking it for granted that superiors would know that they ought not to give unnecessary advice, admonitions, and directives.

The solicitous watchfulness of superiors should never be surveillance. And the importance of a superior's trusting her subjects can scarcely be overstressed. Need we say anything in this context about the disastrous consequences of some actions of superiors, for example, monitoring phone conversations, perusing mail, and other expressions of lack of trust? But if the younger persons are trusted, will not some of them make glaring mistakes? Of course they will.

In fact, I personally do not know of any human being who has never made a mistake. I have, however, known people who seemed never to have done anything at all on their own, who did only what they were given to do. That is the biggest mistake any person could make. One just cannot take all the risks out of life, no matter what is done. The exercise of liberty will always be fraught with risk. The worst error is to seek to remove from another all possibility of her making a mistake by depriving her of the exercise of her liberty. It is possible to do something which approximates that in religious life, from the well-intentioned motive of avoiding embarrassing mistakes.

A mistake in the one who makes it implies the opportunity to exercise personal responsibility. If, whenever a religious does anything of any consequence, she is merely carrying out someone else's decision, then should something go wrong, the mistake is not imputed to her. It is someone else's mistake. At no time was this her own idea; at no time was this her own decision. She was, in effect, an "errand boy."

If a sister has always followed such a pattern in the more important activities of her religious life, who is to answer for the fact that she has not become a responsible person? Is she to answer for it? She has been denied the opportunity to grow into responsible adulthood. She has not been permitted to exercise in any notable way her prudential judgment. She has failed to learn responsibility from experience because she has not been given responsibilities. The dreadful fact is that in the area of doing her own thinking and deciding she has been kept a child.

Sisters, while listening to these words, "Blessed are the meek," how many of us have reflected that unless we are meek, really self-controlled, we might take over the responsibilities proper to those under us? We might not permit them to run the risk of making mistakes. We might, unwittingly, prevent them from growing into full-fledged, self-accountable adults. One almost wonders, when one sees persons thus damaged, why our Lord did not say "Another commandment I give you, that you respect the right of others to do their own thinking and deciding."

Of course, true meekness on the part of superiors presupposes a real trustworthiness on the part of subjects. Trustworthiness is a rather far-reaching virtue. It does not mean just that subjects can be trusted to make reasonably good judgments; it is also saying that they can be relied upon to act according to these judgments. Moreover, unless subjects are truly considerate of other persons they are not being fully trustworthy. Their trustworthiness includes their loyalty to others and perhaps particularly to their superiors.

The independence which flows from the superior's proper permissiveness is a dependent independence. Clearly all such independence is to be exercised under the overall governance of the superior. Without a basic loyalty to the superior the fitting exercise of such independence becomes an impossibility. I might put it this way: no matter how much independence I am granted in religious life, I should always exercise it according to the known or interpreted will of my superior. After all, it is my superior who alone has the duty of final responsibility for the community itself and for the governing of each of its members. To the extent that an intelligent superior feels personally adequate, she will make sure that she is not running some kind of religious hot-house, in which everyone is "sheltered" from normal, healthy growth.

Meekness in granting one the fullest liberty and trust and corresponding trustworthiness can function only when the superior-subject relationship is as it should be. This right relationship presupposes in the superior a personal respect for each of her subjects and in them a loyalty and considerateness towards her and towards each other. I said a moment ago that the proper independence of subjects is a dependent one, since it is always subject to the superior's authority. Need I make explicit what has already been implied, that the adequate superior is one who knows how to delegate properly?

Subjects need to find in their superior certain qualities. They need to find in her trust and understanding. They need especially her love. At times they will need her strength and they will need her protection. As we have already indicated, meekness implies controlled strength, not its absence.

There are times and circumstances where the superior in order to be meek must show her strength. Such a situation could be one calling for her becoming protection. Sometimes such protection is needed by religious subjects, particularly because the very nature of religious life makes them peculiarly vulnerable to the unreasonable demands from parents, priests, or others upon their time and activities. The adequate superior will permit no one to take advantage of any of her sisters. A given sister may *need* to be able to say to people, "My superior has directed me not to do this."

Fr. Christoph: In the Sermon on the Mount, Christ, after pronouncing each of the Beatitudes, promised a reward for its observance. It is significant that for meekness he said, "They shall possess the earth." In the rewards promised for living the other Beatitudes there is a suggestion that it will be only in the after life that these rewards will be enjoyed. But for those who are meek there is a promise in time of a foretaste of eternal beatitude. The disciplined behavior of the meek, their refusal to return evil for evil, and their gentle manner make them attractive. As the early Fathers wrote, with love as their only weapon the meek are able to win the hearts of men. They are loved and admired by their fellowmen, and most of all their example encourages to holy emulation.

Let us attend to one of the other Beatitudes, "Blessed are the poor in spirit," and put this in the context of the vow and the virtue of poverty. As religious we have at our disposal all kinds of material goods. The Holy See is becoming increasingly concerned about the lack of a spirit of and genuine attachment to poverty. In the Vatican II document on religious life, the Conciliar Fathers have called our attention to the fact that religious must be witnesses to the poverty of Christ by leading a life of poverty.

We must distinguish between collective poverty and personal poverty, both of which normally are governed by rule. Collective poverty demands that as religious we do not have the quantity and quality of material goods that suggests a life of comparative ease. What the community has for its own use, as distinguished from what it may have for externs, should reflect a detachment from wealth, exaggerated comfort, and luxury. Personal poverty is protected by the vow. The vow of poverty says that we cannot call anything our own, and the practice of personal poverty demands that we seek permission for the things we need. In this we are to refrain from asking for what is superfluous.

The virtue of poverty goes further and induces the real woman in religious life to be satisfied with that which is the meanest in the house. In order to have the genuine spirit of poverty we should not only be poor in fact but also be content to be witnesses of Christ in an area where it is so easy to justify almost any piece of equipment or gadget for our personal use on the basis of necessity, efficiency, or urbanity. This is even more necessary in our era which needs the example of genuine detachment from worldly goods.

Fr. Evoy: Poverty of spirit is by no means confined to material things. A contemporary writer has aptly characterized poverty of spirit as "detached attachment."

Implicit in this notion of "detached attachment" are several elements. One is a real care for the persons with whom I am working and living. You do not live very long in religious life before discovering that physical closeness does not need to be personal closeness.

A religious might conscientiously put in long hours in the presence of persons with whom she lives and works and still never let them get really close to her. This means that she would not let herself really care about these persons. She would in this way be maintaining herself secure against any kind of obligating involvement as well as against the kind of hurt that could come only from those for whom she cares. It is important to note, however, that no matter how well she would simulate a personal closeness to others, while remaining thus safely withdrawn from them, she simply would not be having a highly personal impact on these persons. True poverty of spirit would dictate that even though it would leave her liable to be hurt, she would nevertheless permit herself to become rightly and deeply attached to people.

Another element is that of her involvement in her work. She can diminish the suffering that can be anticipated in the prospect of her being removed from a specific area of work by never allowing herself to become really involved in that work. Once again, true poverty of spirit would impel her to throw herself as completely as possible into her work. This she would do with full awareness of her resulting vulnerability to disappointment and hurt from her subsequent removal from that work by those in authority. This risk she accepts for Christ.

Still another element in the "detached attachment" of a woman religious is her underlying willingness to be removed, even suddenly, from the persons who have come to mean so much to her. In fact, the perfection of poverty of spirit might even urge a religious, after she had fully informed her superior about the matter, to reassure the latter of her willingness to be assigned on a mission or work with a sister whom she found very difficult.

Again the readiness to be removed from a particular work or from any facility or instrument associated with that work should characterize her poverty of spirit. And this would not require that she agree to the wisdom of such a removal. She thus finds herself without unwholesome attachment to any person or thing.

Moreover, her poverty of spirit would make it simply unthinkable for her to say to her superior, "I do not care where I am placed or what I am given to do as long as I am assured of security, or as long as I am left in this part of the country, or provided I am allowed to remain in this specific work." She knows there were no such clauses in fine print at the bottom of her vow formula. In her yearning to live completely for Christ she will give herself wholly, while fully prepared under the operation of religious obedience to accept as from God whatever changes her superiors direct her to make.

If my own superior tomorrow assigned me to work on one of the Indian missions, I do not mind telling you that I would not like it. In fact, I would consider it an unwise assignment for me, in view of the investment the Society has made to educate me for another field of work. If after listening to whatever reasons my superior gave, I still thought it was unwise, I would respectfully tell my superior what my thinking was. After having heard what I had to say on the matter, should he say, "Nevertheless, I want you to go to the Indian mission," I would go. Unless I then went,

I would not have the "detached attachment" of true poverty of spirit.

Fr. Christoph: Not only would he go but I do not think that he would lose his composure in conforming to the will of the superior. He would not become a nervous wreck, because while he has an attachment to his work, it is the type of attachment from which, for the love of God, he can be separated.

If my superior came around tomorrow and said, "I want you to become an assistant pastor at St. X Church," I think I would say, "I do not think this is a wise use of my talents and preparation, but if that is what you want, that is what I do." I won't like it, but that does not become a factor in my behavior. If superiors choose to use us unwisely, they have to answer for the way they may have neglected to use our talents. But we should never be so attached to any kind of activity that our degree of involvement renders it impossible for us to be obedient.

Fr. Evoy: We are not presenting a treatment of obedience at this time. Our concern here is only with the "detached attachment" proper to poverty of spirit. When St. Ignatius in his well-known letter of obedience says that a religious should be like a dead body or an old man's staff, he was referring to the resistance a subject would offer to an order of obedience. Applying this to the above example, after the superior who understood my case said, "Nevertheless, I want you to go to the Indian mission," I would hope to offer no more resistance than would a dead body or an old man's staff. I certainly would not say, "I won't!"

Fr. Christoph: The subject should make whatever representations he can. The superior should listen to him because in the subject's mind they are reasonable, and he has the right to be heard. Superiors should not frown upon such representations as indicative of insubordination. Then, if the superior is going to act foolishly, he has no one but himself to blame. After the subject is finished with his representing, even though his devout will cannot bend the understanding to accept the superior's position, nevertheless, he says, "You are the boss; you call the shots. Do I go to the Indian mission or don't I?" And the Superior says, "Father, you go to the mission." Now he is the cadaver. Now he is the old man's staff. But he has done no violence to himself in submitting to authority.

Fr. Evoy: Poverty of spirit when seen in proper perspective is nothing more or less than openness to God's love. It is the keeping of ourselves free so as to maintain a high degree of mobility. In a word, it is a striving for a "detached attachment" which would leave us the maximum freedom for the most effective service of our King.

14 *The Call*

Fr. Christoph: Since we have long ago made our religious commitment, we shall reflect upon our vocation with a view to discovering to what extent we have thus far fulfilled it.

Recall the circumstances of the calling of the first Apostles. Christ was walking by the Sea of Galilee. He saw Simon and his brother Andrew casting a net into the sea and he said, "Come follow me and I will make you fishers of men." And Matthew tells us that they left their nets at once and followed him. Later he saw two others, James the son of Zebedee and his brother John, mending their nets, and he invited them. They left their nets and their father to follow him. On another occasion when Christ was passing by, he saw Levi and to him he said, "Follow me," and Levi promptly left his tax table to give himself to the mission of Christ.

In the Acts we read about the vocation of another Apostle. Thrown from his horse as he was drawing near to Damascus, and temporarily blinded, he heard a voice saying, "Saul, Saul, why dost thou persecute me?" And Saul asked, "Who art thou, Lord?" And when Christ identified himself, Saul said, "Lord, what wilt thou have me do?" He then, without any hesitation, carried out the directives of Christ, completely, exactly, immediately. We all know him as the great St. Paul.

These passages of Sacred Scripture show us, indeed, how whole-heartedly the response to the call of Christ can be. And the subsequent history of these same men show also how perfectly the commitment to Christ can be kept. The generosity of the Apostles is joined to the grace of God, which in the last analysis is always present so that man is able to satisfy the obligations inherent in so sublime a calling.

You will notice that in the invitation of Christ to the Apostles and in their acceptance there is a common pattern. To each, Christ freely presents an invitation, not a command. On the part of the Apostles there is the unreserved, unhesitating, and complete giving of selves to Christ—no holding back. There is no evidence of hedging against the possibility of failure in the future. As far as we know, not one of these Apostles harbored the thought "I will save a little something for myself just in case this does not work out." These first Apostles of Christ knew something about the man, his techniques and his mission. There is no evidence that the Apostles had more than a vague idea where Christ himself would go, where he would lead them, what he would expect of them, and what he would demand of them. And yet, despite this, they trusted Christ so much that they were able to give themselves unreservedly to him and to his cause.

When you pronounced your vows you had in mind to give Christ everything. The presumption was that your commitment was wholehearted. Looking back upon life in religion up to this present moment, there might be a realization that you have not retained the generosity of your original commitment. You could be amazed, chagrined, or humiliated to discover that you have saved something for yourself. Father Evoy recalled the example of Sapphira and Ananias. There must have been some lingering doubt that if they gave all, sooner or later they might regret it, because they did retain some of their wealth.

Could it be that after having given yourselves unreservedly on your vow day, you had some second thoughts later on regarding the totality of your commitment? Could it be that you looked at others and saw an unacceptable mediocrity and so became afraid to trust yourself completely to God, lest you would meet with a similar fate—bogged down in the same unpalatable mediocrity? As time went on you too began to hedge against such a future by withdrawing part of your commitment from Christ. Should such be the case you should be somewhat uncomfortable. Vocation reaches its highest perfection and gives its greatest satisfaction when one gives herself to Christ without reservation.

Fr. Evoy: Father Christoph's remarks on vocation remind me that there has been a change in the value placed by many on a religious vocation. The change is exemplified by the remark a Catholic woman repeated to both of us recently. She had been talking to an elderly sister who was upset at the many changes taking place in religious life. Of particular concern to this sister was the possible introduction of a radically different religious garb. And the telltale remark then came out. "What do they expect us to do," she asked with apprehension, "dress like common laywomen?"

That question reveals an attitude that was all too common for some years in the Church. It implied that the cream of Catholic womanhood was skimmed off into religious life, while the rejects stayed in the world. This, of course, is a blunt wording of the attitude in question. Those women, it was explained, whom God had especially chosen for religious life became sisters and those who were not so selected, along with those who did not heed "the call," entered the state of marriage or remained single. Regardless of the wording, the attitude was unmistakable. It said that the highest calling for anyone was religious life.

Matrimony was pictured as considerably below this lofty religious calling. It is strange that the pendulum has swung over until it is now well on the other side. Catholic marriage is no longer in the position of having to give a justification for itself. Quite the opposite. It is religious life which is now coming under attack. Because of the many contemporary writings extolling the sacredness of marriage, questions are raised in regard to the justification for religious life.

Among the defenses that have been made for religious life are some that damn it with faint praise. For instance, some place is conceded to religious in the present onward thrust of salvation history. It is the place of religious, it has been said, to hold, in reasonable comfort and security, the home "fort" so as to free the nonreligious for the truly adventuresome works of apostolic zeal. In the knowledge that the "home guard" is on the job, the laity can venture forth at great personal sacrifice and hardship, carrying the good news of the Gospel throughout the world. These committed lay people will dare to bring Christ to his own anywhere on earth. You suspect immediately that such an explanation is out near the other end of the pendulum's swing. Nevertheless, such a slanted explanation does point up the need for an adequate answer to the question, "Why religious life?"

And while the limitations of time here will not permit anything approaching an adequate treatise on the true reasons for religious life, it is of the utmost importance that we at least indicate some of the grounds for justifying its existence. In your voluntary renunciation of the tremendous possibilities of married life for this immediate dedication of yourselves to Christ, you must fully know why this dedication under vows to God is eminently and wonderfully worthwhile. In undertaking such an account we must be extremely careful not to give incorrect reasons.

Among the wrong reasons given is that of justifying religious life primarily on the basis of the work done by religious. History can be misleading here, for it happens to be a fact that many areas of work, such as nursing, social work, and teaching, were originally done exclusively by religious. Obviously this is no longer true. No contemporary religious can feel confident that she could not be replaced in her work by a lay person. This would mean, in fact, that were she to give her work as the primary reason for her religious life, she would be justified being in that life only as long as her work could not be done by someone who was not a religious.

To begin with, your commitment, made under vows to Almighty God and received by him through the instrumentality of his Church, carols forth the value of the gift of yourself, as a person, regardless of any and every other value you might have. Surprisingly, it is precisely on this score that your married sister needs you badly. In fact, you become her reassurance that she can rightly rest the solidity of her married life on the value of being a woman in her own right, aside from every other consideration. In marriage a woman needs to know that she is valued and loved first and foremost as a person. There have, unfortunately, been times when women, both in and out of marriage, have been valued almost exclusively in terms of their ability to produce offspring, or pleasure, or for some such other reason. The value of a woman must never be rated primarily in terms of her ability to satisfy, on any score, her husband, or anyone else for that matter.

Any evaluation of a person *as* a person, primarily in terms of her accomplishments, is an abomination. I recall an experience of mine in which this attitude was exemplified. I was introduced to a well-known European priest-psychologist. He shook my hand, looked into my face and asked immediately, "What have you written?" These were his opening words. They expressed to me what I regard as a not uncommon attitude of our day, namely, reckoning the worth of a person principally on the basis of his achievements.

Your religious life trumpets forth the truth that a woman as a person in her own right possesses a value most acceptable to Almighty God and is therefore worthwhile. She is valuable by reason of her intrinsic human dignity, aside from her potential

motherhood, her ability to satisfy a man, and any such consideration.

Many a married woman, whether she ever explicitly tells herself so or not, nonetheless *needs* to be able to point to you for the
living proof that a woman is valuable in her own right because
she is a woman. She does not *have* to produce children. She does
not *have* to do anything other than to be what she really ought
to be—a genuine woman—in order to be of real value. Successful
marriage implies the mutual love and respect of two persons. Accordingly, a woman knows that only if her married life is built
on reverence for her own person, as one loved and cherished in
her own right, will motherhood be to her a most glorious experience. Surprisingly enough, the fact that marriage and motherhood, rightly viewed, are seen to be so wonderful is what makes
your impact so great.

Sisters, when you walk down the street, you are seen by people
who do not at all understand what motivates your life. Some are
going to be openly cynical, smiling at your profession of voluntary celibacy. But whatever their reaction, they do not for a
moment miss what you are saying by your way of life. Your
presence itself is a constant reminder, welcome or not, of the
for-God-ness of this world. Just by being seen, you proclaim to
people the transcendence of God. Your very existence professes
that in this whole world God is first and foremost.

Fr. Christoph: The cynicism among some non-Catholics regarding the value of religious life is disappearing. Non-Catholics may
have some doubts and may wonder, but there are too many of
you for them to ignore. You force them to reflect. You are a
mighty phalanx saying, *"we are God's."* And as Father Evoy says,
this serves notice to all that man must love not merely for time
but for eternity. Moreover, you stand out as significantly sacrifi-
cial. You, in a sense, emphasize and prove to the world that there
are values other than the purely temporal. When she lists the

people who are in heaven, it is not without reason that the
Church joins the virgins to the martyrs because there is a genuine
martyrdom in what virginity implies.

You are uncommitted to any individual person; therefore, you
can be approached by all mankind. The married woman is committed primarily to one man and to her family. Your second vow
releases you from the confines of the matrimonial hearth and
leaves you open to serve God in various ways.

Fr. Evoy: Man will always be in need of reminders of the
for-God-ness of the universe. Despite this world's many evils it is
nevertheless replete with the beautiful. Human beings can perceive the beautiful which is present and become entranced by it.
This is good. But people can become so preoccupied with it, that
this beauty can lose its transparency. They might fail to see
through it to the source of all beauty, the Triune God. They can
come to a dead leveling off of all being, according to which everything is viewed as exclusively horizontal. From such a vantage
point, everything begins at the level of the perceptible universe
and ends up on the same plane.

These persons have lost sight of the vertical. They have forgotten that the existence and movement of this world is from God.
Lost sight of is the all-important truth that everything that exists
is destined through the mediation of man to be returned to God.
People need to be reminded of the vertical dimension—the *from-
God-ness* and *for-God-ness* of the world. And human nature being
inclined as it is, people *always* will need to be reminded of that
vertical all-significant dimension.

Your life is a *sign* to all of this vertical dimension. For them
just to encounter you is to be confronted with the reminder of
God's important place in the universe. Precisely as a sign or symbol, you constantly remind man of this primacy.

But cannot a married woman reach the heights of holiness?
Most certainly. Does she not, equally with the religious, stand

forth as a sign reminding man of God? No, for she is not seen directly as a sign or symbol. Nonetheless, a tremendous woman in the lay state will eventually communicate her attitude towards God to all who really get to know her. But she appears first of all as another woman, not primarily as a sign pointing directly to God. There are real women who have no conscious desire to lead men to God. And yet even these, when really known, quite unwittingly say something about God to a truly insightful person.

On the other hand, a sister appears, at first glance, not merely as another woman. Her religious garb comes across to onlookers with all the impact of a neon sign pointing Godward. Your religous life is symbolized to other people through your distinctively religious dress. At a glance, a woman in the lay state says to others that she is this *woman*. At a glance, you say to others that you are this *sister*. Your single or married sister is seen by others as first of all a person in her own right. While you remain a person in your own right, you are seen immediately as a woman especially dedicated to God. Sisters, you are a sign of *for-God-ness* to others.

You are also, or certainly should be, the spokesman to every person with whom you come in contact that God cares about that person, that God personally loves that individual. Note now that because you are living signs of the importance of God's place in the world, simply by being present among men you can symbolize God's interest, without needing to do any particular thing to demonstrate this interest.

But to be a sign to people of God's *love*, you must indeed do something. You must *love* people with a warm, strong, pure, becoming, real woman's love. When you thus genuinely love another, that person does not see this just as the love of a woman, but rather as the love of this consecrated woman. Such love can bespeak the reality of God's love as would few other manifestations.

It is of the utmost importance that we spell this out in a

practical way here. To the extent that you have time for and really care about those with whom you come in contact, so does Christ. You bring them evidence of the reality of Christ's love for them. Whether you realize it or not, they see your love and concern as his love and concern. For many persons, as you go, so goes Christ. What a tremendous opportunity and awe-inspiring responsibility your vocation is.

Fr. Christoph: Father Evoy remarked that those defending marriage as against the religious state are very vocal today. The very thoughtful and theologically correct treatises and essays on the sacrament of marriage have called the attention of all to the greatness of the vocation to the married state. These works are read by religious. And with a somewhat confused understanding of her own vocation, a sister may think, "Perhaps I should get married and *do the work of God* and let the religious be symbols." Such thinking betrays a lack of appreciation for religious life. You are doing God's work in the community to which you have given yourself. Over and above your value as symbols, as Father Evoy has pointed out, is the worth of your way of life in itself.

Since your rules and constitutions bear the mark of the Church's approval, you have the most cogent assurance that your way of life has value in God's eyes. Truly, if there were no other reason to justify your existence as religious, this would be sufficient. If as a real woman you were a religious all alone on an island, your way of life would have a value in the eyes of God, because you would be giving glory to God in a uniquely and most immediately personal way.

Fr. Evoy: This immediate gift of yourselves to Christ under religious vows is most worthwhile. This free choice of a life of dedicated virginity for God in a religious community, in preference to the magnificent way of life marriage could be, is of itself something of great value. Every other love you have will always be a true love if kept properly within the framework of your love for Christ.

Fr. Christoph: I would like to develop further our earlier remark about the actual living out of the commitment inherent in religious vocation. A religious ought not to stand still in religious life. She should grow in it. As you make progress in the religious state, you see that you have to slough off this, that, and the other attachment which you, at one time, thought so important for your material or spiritual well-being.

We turn to the Apostles for encouragement because their lives tell us how to be happy in the service of Christ. Jesus called these twelve men to him and, as far as we can see, their break with whatever in the past was incompatible with their new calling was complete. Their dedication to Christ, too, was equally complete. Their lives tell us, among other things, that we can only be happy in the service of God when we are sincerely generous.

Hence you ought to ask yourself seriously the question, "What stands in the way of my total surrender to Christ? Am I too attached to anything?" It might be your pride, your egotism, your sensitivity, or any other undesirable personality trait that stands in the way of your complete dedication. A place, a person, or a thing might have the power to prevent or at least distract you from living your commitment to Christ completely.

Fr. Evoy: I think it is Gustave Thibon who maintains that one of the things that many of us cling to and find most difficult to give up is our own peculiar notion of God. We can remain largely unaware that we are not open to the Holy Spirit. We can assume that he just *has* to act towards us in a certain way. So often, we do not identify operations as his, unless they follow the pattern of our expectations of the way God should act.

Fr. Christoph: I suspect that this is a problem more often found among women than men. Women can become very angry with God. Their concept of God as good, merciful, generous, and the like does not always measure up to their expectations. As a consequence they may become depressed and discouraged and sometimes even despair because they are so often concerned about a God whom their imagination has created. God's providence in their regard does not fit in with their distorted preconceptions.

Fr. Evoy: I find Father Christoph's remark that females get very angry with God interesting. They do. Seldom do we hear a man say he is mad at God. So many females say it because they are. Is it not amazing that a person can say she loves God and still insist on dictating to him the rules according to which he is to act? Not one of you, I believe, would say to God, "Meet my specifications in the matter of how and what you do, and I will love you; otherwise I am angry with you." Nevertheless, some of you might feel that were you to be completely honest with yourself, you ought to say it. How else would you explain your getting angry at God? Is it not that you feel he is not playing fair because he is not playing by *your* rules? Your firm hold on this conviction could be your one great inordinate attachment. It would simply mean that you could not leave yourself fully open to the Holy Spirit.

This suggests a point which I think calls for some consideration. If you can do this to God, is it so astonishing that you could also do it to people? Sisters, you have no genuine love for another unless you are perfectly willing to let that other person be herself. The insistence that you will love this individual, if she will change to what you are sure she should be, is something else masquerading as love. It surely is not genuine love.

You can tell yourself you will love this sister if she will stop doing that most annoying thing and become her best self according to your blueprint for her. If she becomes that, you will love her. Because you want to love her, you will never rest until she becomes what you "know" she should be. You ask, "Isn't that the way God loves her? Does he not insist also, because he loves her, that she become her best self?"

No. He wants her to be her best self—that is true. But he loves her with a love that respects her freedom so completely as to allow her to be the way she freely chooses to be. This holds true even if she refuses to return his love. He could not say to her, "I will love you *if* you will do such and such." There are no "ifs" in God's love for her. His love is not contingent upon her behavior, although her love for him is very contingent upon her behavior. But can you say that you will love her on the condition that she shapes up to what you are certain she should be? It is possible that you can go through your religious life for years and never recognize the demanding conditions of your "love."

Recall our Lord's parable of the workers called into the vineyard. The master had agreed to give one denarius to each of those who worked the full day. At the end, these full-day toilers were angry with him. Despite the contract they had made with him, they felt he was unfair in not paying them more than was being given to those who had labored only a short time. The lesson is clear.

I think that in the last analysis, one of the greatest single deterrents to charity in religious life can be that you might have norms according to which both God and your sisters *have* to act. Otherwise you are disappointed and angry. And all the while, you can be utterly unaware that you are making any such demands on either God or your sisters. Meanwhile God's unconditional love is your model for loving both him and your sisters.

15   *Lazarus—Friend of Christ*

Fr. Christoph: The study and imitation of Christ is to be your life work, Sisters. Since you are going to follow him who is "the way, the truth, and the life," you ought to know more and more about him. That is why your daily meditation, for the most part, should find its inspiration in the Gospel accounts of his life. We obviously have to be selective in the choice of the episodes in the life of Christ upon which we reflect. In view of the very important lessons we can learn from it, we will consider a most touching story found in the eleventh chapter of St. John's Gospel.

> Now a certain man was sick, Lazarus of Bethany, the village of Mary and her sister Martha. Now it was Mary who anointed the Lord with ointment and wiped his feet dry with her hair, whose brother Lazarus was sick. The sisters therefore sent to him, saying, "Lord, behold, he whom thou lovest is sick."
>
> But when Jesus heard this, he said to them, "This sickness is not unto death, but for the glory of God, that through it the Son of God may be glorified." Now Jesus loved Martha and her sister Mary, and Lazarus. So when he heard that he was sick, he remained two more days in the same place.

Then afterwards he said to his disciples, "Let us go again into Judea."

The disciples said to him, "Rabbi, just now the Jews were seeking to stone thee; and dost thou go there again?" Jesus answered, "Are there not twelve hours in the day? If a man walks in the day, he does not stumble, because he seeks the light of this world. But if he walks in the night, he stumbles, because the light is not in him."

These things he spoke, and after this he said to them, "Lazarus, our friend, sleeps. But I go that I may wake him up from sleep." His disciples therefore said, "Lord, if he sleeps, he will be safe." Now Jesus had spoken of his death, but they thought he was speaking of the repose of sleep. So then Jesus said to them plainly, "Lazarus is dead; and I rejoice on your account that I was not there, that you may believe. But let us go to him." Thomas, who is called the Twin, said therefore to his fellow-disciples, "Let us also go, that we may die with him."

Jesus therefore came and found him already four days in the tomb. Now Bethany was close to Jerusalem, some fifteen stadia distant. And many of the Jews had come to Mary and Martha to comfort them on account of their brother. When, therefore, Martha heard that Jesus was coming, she went to meet him. But Mary remained at home.

Martha therefore said to Jesus, "Lord, if thou hadst been here my brother would not have died. But even now I know that whatever thou shalt ask of God, God will give it to thee."

Jesus said to her, "Thy brother shall rise." Martha said to him, "I know that he will rise at the resurrection, on the last day." Jesus said to her, "I am the resurrection and the life; he who believes in me, even if he die, shall live; and whoever lives and believes in me, shall never die. Dost thou believe this?" She said to him, "Yes, Lord, I believe that thou art the Christ, the Son of God, who is come into the world."

And when she said this, she went away and quietly called Mary her sister, saying, "The Master is here and calls thee." As soon as she heard this, she rose quickly and came to him, for Jesus had not yet come into the village, but was still at the place where Martha had met him.

When, therefore, the Jews, who were with her in the house and were comforting her, saw Mary rise up quickly and go out, they followed her, saying, "She is going to the tomb to weep there."

When, therefore, Mary came where Jesus was, and saw him, she fell at his feet, and said to him, "Lord, if thou hadst been here, my brother would not have died." When, therefore, Jesus saw her weeping, and the Jews who had come with her weeping, he groaned in spirit and was troubled, and said, "Where have you laid him?" They said to him, "Lord, come and see." And Jesus wept. The Jews therefore said, "See how he loved him." But some of them said, "Could not he who opened the eyes of the blind, have caused that this man should not die?"

Jesus therefore, again groaning in himself, came to the tomb. Now it was a cave, and a stone was laid against it. Jesus said, "Take away the stone." Martha, the sister of him who was dead, said to him, "Lord, by this time he is already decayed, for he is dead four days." Jesus said to her, "Have I not told thee that if thou believe thou shalt behold the glory of God?" They therefore removed the stone. And Jesus, raising his eyes, said, "Father, I give thee thanks that thou hast heard me. Yet I knew that thou always hearest me; but because of the people who stand around, I spoke, that they may believe that thou hast sent me." When he had said this, he cried out with a loud voice, "Lazarus, come forth!" And at once he who had been dead came forth, bound feet and hands with bandages, and his face was tied up with a cloth. Jesus said to them, "Unbind him, and let him go." (John 11:1–44.)

This touching account of the restoring of Lazarus to life makes us peculiarly aware of the humanness of Christ. God is intangible because he is pure spirit and as such cannot be our visible model. After the Fall and its consequences and God's determination to redeem man, there is a fittingness in the Incarnation. God tells us, "Walk before me and be perfect." Because we are human we need a model with "skin on." So Almighty God, the Second Person of the Trinity, has taken upon himself our human nature. Now we can love him in his humanity because he loves us with his humanity.

He has experienced the emotions that you experience to show you how to use your emotions and employ them for his glory. He wanted to teach you by his own example the value and the correct use of feelings. As you follow him throughout his life, you see him sorrowing with the sorrowful, rejoicing with the joyful, loving others with true human love. Indeed he appears to experience all the emotions which color your own life. How intensely human Christ is in this episode! Before he approached the tomb of Lazarus, Christ wept. He was unashamedly sorrowful because he loved.

It is significant that God would have to become man if he would experience our kind of love. Again and again, he shows the warmth of human affection. Jesus loved Mary, Martha, and Lazarus. He loved each one of them in a singular way because each one of them was a unique person with a loveableness not completely identifiable with the loveableness of any other.

Fr. Evoy: I think some of you will recall that Martin Buber, the philosopher, used this very example of the raising of Lazarus to illustrate something about human love. Buber stated that while human love is never essentially made up of feelings, it is nevertheless always associated with them. In addition, he said that while no one would question the genuineness of Christ's love for Mary, Martha and Lazarus, neither would anyone suggest that Christ's feelings were identical in each instance. It would be preposterous, Buber pointed out, to hold that his feelings of personal love for Mary were exactly the same as those he had for Lazarus or Martha. Father Christoph's point is that in our Lord's love he has feelings proper both to himself and appropriate to the one loved. His love of each of you is, therefore, intensely personal. He does not feel about you exactly as he feels about anyone else!

Fr. Christoph: This highly personalized aspect of Christ's love is extremely important. You see a person; you hear a voice; you observe an action. As a result you find individuals attractive to you. This attraction may lead to love, and the kind of love you experience will vary with each individual towards whom you are drawn. In Christian literature and Christian asceticism, Mary Magdalene has been portrayed as the model of the contemplative and Martha as the model of those whose love of God moves them to serve him in their neighbor. Christ's attitude towards Mary Magdalene would be somewhat different from his attitude toward Martha. They were two different persons. The affection between Christ and Lazarus is different again. It represents to us the nobility of human friendship which one can have for another of the same sex.

I want to repeat what has already been said. You cannot make anyone love you, although you may want her affection and love. Though you are a real woman, you may not possess the particular kind of personality towards which this individual is attracted. Just because you are drawn to her does not mean that she is necessarily drawn to you. There is little that you can do about this. She will simply not be your close friend. You must choose your intimates from among the available and willing. It is significant that Christ also had his intimate friends.

Of his Apostles, Peter, James, and John stood out as his closest friends; and John, as the one he loved. Not indeed that he did not love the rest, but his relationship with John was a unique intimacy that set John off from the rest. In the case of the other disciples, of whom there must have been hundreds, it would seem that Christ was closest to Mary, Martha, and Lazarus. Just as Christ did not love all with the same love, neither can you love all with the same love. And just as Christ counted a small group as his intimate friends, so too you will find that you will have only a small group of intimate friends.

Fr. Evoy: There is a most interesting application here of a point we were speaking about earlier. As our Lord approached Bethany, Martha got word of it and hurried out to meet him. She said to Christ, "If you had been present, my brother Lazarus would not have died." She then went immediately to tell her sister. And Mary, when she encountered Christ, said practically the same thing to him. She began, "If you had been here . . ." Both these women were saying in effect, "We sent you word that Lazarus was very ill. So, why did you not come?" They did not come right out and tell him how dreadfully he had disappointed them in their hour of need. They simply repeated that if he had been present, this unspeakably painful tragedy would never have occurred. And while they were saying this to him, they were aware that he knew they had sent him word in plenty of time.

When he reached the sepulcher, our Lord prayed openly, "Father, I give thee thanks that thou hast heard me. Yet I know that thou always hearest me." This prayer was also an answer to the implicit accusation of Mary and Martha that if his love had been great enough, Lazarus would not have died. Was he not, in effect, saying to these two sisters, "Should it not have been enough for you that you made sure I knew? Could you not trust my love? Could you not be receptive to my way of responding to your plea?"

You should be able to appreciate the feelings of Mary and Martha. They loved their brother. They felt, therefore, that because our Lord loved him and them, he simply would not let Lazarus die. Yet, who said that this was the way Christ had to show his love? The sisterly love of Mary and Martha called for it to be shown that way. Only later did these two women come to see that Christ's manner of showing his love was the better way. Our Lord thus gave not only a greater manifestation of his love to the three of them but a beautiful tribute to Lazarus as well.

Fr. Christoph: Out of love for Mary, Martha, and Lazarus, Christ called Lazarus back from death. But he did it also to prove that he was God. "Because of the people who stood around, I spoke that they may believe that thou hast sent me." In the mind of Christ this was an opportunity to do something to prove his love for his close friends and also to prove to all mankind down the ages that he has power over life and death.

Fr. Evoy: The attitude of Mary and Martha towards our Lord, when their brother died, is one into which a sister can slip. It is at times possible for her to feel, "God does not appear to hear me. I tell him but he does not seem to listen." She "knows" that if he were really listening, he would do what she asks him to do. Without being aware of it, such a sister can thus tend to restrict the freedom of God in his dealings with her, by assuming that her way of doing something is the only way of doing it.

It is so important to remind yourselves from time to time that God does love each of you personally. And when you tell him of your needs and those of others for whom you care, he does listen. Moreover, you can be sure that he will do everything his love for you urges him to do. And although you might ask him to do it a certain way, this should always be far removed from a demand that he do it that way.

Fr. Christoph: To the friends of Lazarus the behavior of Christ was incomprehensible. If he loved Lazarus enough to weep over his death, why did he not prevent that death? They voiced their disappointment in the question "Could not he who opened the eyes of the blind have caused that this man should not die?" The purpose of Christ's action escaped the understanding of his followers. And yet it is obvious now that Christ's way of acting showed him to be most wise. Here we have an example of the universal tendency for man to see things only from his own perspective.

You should be aware of this tendency in yourselves in your criticisms of others. Is it not true that for the most part you expect everyone to function according to your view of the situation? You ask, "Why did not Sister Superior do this? Why did not Sister Mary do this other thing?" You reflect in this manner because you are looking at reality from your own point of view, and this is understandable. For you this is realistic. But should you not be willing to admit that there is another viewpoint? In counseling married couples I suggest alternate views— "There is your side," I say to one; "There is your side," I say to the other; "and there is the right side." And this last may not correspond to either of the positions held by the spouses.

My glasses, which I am holding in my hand, are both concave and convex. Looking at them from this side, I say that they are concave. I am unable to see the other side because of the way I am holding them. Father Evoy looks at them and says with equal truth that from his point of view they are convex. This points up a lesson for you. Often it is the point of view rather than the reality which gives rise to opposing positions so harmful to interpersonal relationships. Your viewpoint as colored by passion, personal background, environmental factors, health, prejudice, age, role, and the like so often prevents you from seeing what is objectively there.

An appreciation of this fact should make you ever so much more tolerant of the opinions, beliefs, attitudes, and behavior of others. Try to recognize the many facets of any situation and to realize that your way of looking at it is but one way. Sometimes the mutual recognition of the other's point of view may facilitate agreement or compromise. You should not be so wedded to your point of view that you become the sun in the universe—so that everything must revolve around you. This is, in effect, what you do when you want God to shape the universe, to perform even miracles, to control the destinies of men, and especially of your companions and yourself in a manner that meets your expectations.

Fr. Evoy: Notice the *symbolism* in Christ's recalling Lazarus from the dead. Our Lord said Lazarus "sleeps." Is bodily death not a sleep when compared with mortal sin, the true death of the soul? In recalling Lazarus to life our Lord was signifying, in a most striking fashion, that he is able to call one back from the death of the soul. Through this recall of Lazarus from bodily death he was in striking fashion symbolizing his power to raise a person from the death of mortal sin. And Christ left us in no doubt that mortal sin is complete death. Recall that he had cautioned his disciples against the devil precisely because the latter could manage an effect far greater than bodily death—that of leading a person into eternal destruction.

Fr. Christoph: In his conversation with Martha, Christ made a remarkable promise. "He who believes in me," he said, "shall live." It would be wrong to conclude from this that merely an act of faith in Christ would guarantee eternal life. Elsewhere, our Lord said, "Not everyone who says 'Lord, Lord' shall enter the kingdom of heaven; but he that does the will of my Father."

Hence the act of faith about which Christ speaks is an act of *realizing* faith which permeates one's whole life and governs all one's actions. As St. Paul reminds us, "The just man lives *by* faith" and not merely with faith.

Fr. Evoy: Sisters, you live by faith. Hence, ultimately you accept the truths of religion and the worthwhileness of your religious life on the revealed word of God. While the *meaning* of your life is derived directly from faith, its primary *motive* is your love of God. One great expression of your love is your acceptance of faith. How do you know that you are going to be able to make it back to God safely when your earthly life is spent? Your answer—your faith and trust in him.

Fr. Christoph: This is another reason why, every day, you should pray, "Increase thou my faith." In a very real sense, the progress you make in your spiritual life will be proportioned to the degree to which you believe. The act of faith and hope merge into one permeating act of love. Somewhere, Archbishop Goodier has written that the act of faith, repeated meaningfully often enough, transforms itself into an act of love so that one begins by saying sincerely "I believe" and ends up by saying "I love."

16 *Palm Sunday*

Fr. Evoy: Here are the Gospel accounts of Palm Sunday as given in both Matthew and Luke. First, St. Matthew:

> And when they drew near to Jerusalem, and came to Bethphage, on the Mount of Olives, then Jesus sent two disciples, saying to them, "Go into the village opposite you, and immediately you will find an ass tied, and a colt with her; loose them and bring them to me. And if anyone say anything to you, you shall say that the Lord has need of them, and immediately he will send them." Now this was done that what was spoken through the prophet might be fulfilled, *Tell the daughter of Sion: Behold, thy king comes to thee, meek and seated upon an ass, and upon a colt, the foal of a beast of burden.*
>
> So the disciples went and did as Jesus had directed them. And they brought the ass and the colt, laid their cloaks on them, and made him sit thereon. And most of the crowd spread their cloaks upon the road, while others were cutting branches from the trees, and strewing them on the road. And the crowds that went before him, and those that followed, kept crying out, saying, *Hosanna to the Son of*

David! Blessed is he who comes in the name of the Lord!
Hosanna in the highest! And when he entered Jerusalem,
all the city was thrown into commotion, saying, "Who is
this?" But the crowds kept on saying, "This is Jesus the
prophet from Nazareth of Galilee." ((Matt. 21:1–11.)

St. Luke's account:

And it came to pass, when he drew near to Bethphage and
Bethany, at the mountain called Olivet, that he sent two of
his disciples, saying, "Go into the village opposite; on entering it you will find a colt of an ass tied, upon which no
man ever yet sat; loose it and bring it. And if anyone ask
you, 'Why are you loosing it?' you shall answer him thus,
'Because the Lord has need of it.'"

And they who were sent went away and found the colt
standing, even as he had told them. And as they were loosing the colt, its owners said to them, "Why are you loosing
the colt?" And they replied, "Because the Lord has need of
it."

And they brought it to Jesus, and throwing their cloaks
over the colt they set Jesus on it. And as he went, they kept
spreading their cloaks upon the road. And when he was
drawing near, being by now at the descent of the Mount of
Olives, the whole company of the disciples began to rejoice
and to praise God with a loud voice for all the miracles
that they had seen, saying, "Blessed is he who comes as king,
in the name of the Lord! Peace in heaven, and glory in the
highest!"

And some of the Pharisees from the crowds said to him,
"Master, rebuke thy disciples." He said to them, "I tell you
that if these keep silence, the stones will cry out."

And when he drew near and saw the city, he wept over it,
saying, "If thou hadst known, in this thy day, even thou, the

things that are for thy peace! But now they are hidden from
thy eyes. For days will come upon thee when thy enemies
will throw up a rampart about thee, and surround thee and
shut thee in on every side, and will dash thee to the ground
and thy children within thee, and will not leave in thee one
stone upon another, because thou hast not known the time
of thy visitation." (Luke 19:29–44.)

Fr. Christoph: "If thou hadst known, in this thy day, the things
that are for thy peace." It should be a source of personal satisfaction to reflect that your community thinks enough of your spiritual welfare and advancement in perfection to give you the time
in which to evaluate your progress. These are periods of grace
and the use you put them to may well determine your future.
The opportunity that is yours—the quiet, the silence, the whole
atmosphere of the house—all these things are orientated towards
a healthy introspection. You need time to be alone with Christ;
you need freedom from your daily routine to meditate upon
those truths "that are for your peace."

Fr. Evoy: Our Lord's words "I tell you that if these keep silence,
the stones will cry out" suggest some further reflections on religious silence which Father Christoph just mentioned. Some years
ago I noticed, in a laymen's retreat house lobby, a plaque enu-
merating reasons why retreatants should keep silence. It pointed
out that prayer required both concentration and close attention
to God and then went on to explain that both of these were impossible without silence. I remember wondering, at the time, why
incorrect reasons should have had to be given for keeping silence
during retreat. The fact of the matter is that at times concentration and close attention to God are actually greatest, not in
silence, but when persons are praying together or seriously talking together about God.

    To the best of my knowledge, silence has always been an in-
separable part of religious community life. The assumption,

therefore, is that there must have been some good reason for instituting it. So preoccupied, it seems to me, are some of the younger generation with the undeniable benefits of dialogue that there is the likelihood they will summarily strive to discard religious silence completely.

However, this kind of silence ought not simply to be classed as an outdated relic of another age, of necessity to be done away with simply on the score that it has been around for such a long time. Neither, on the other hand, ought it to be held as something necessarily sacrosanct simply because it is old. It might be that the need which there was for silence in the past, would not be present today. At any rate, it is at least debatable that contemporary religious are really less in need of religious silence than were religious in previous times. Nevertheless, it appears highly improbable that there is no need whatever for religious silence today. Silence is often an inseparable condition of one's personal prayer.

Fr. Christoph: You want to communicate privately with God at times. This is especially true when your problem is a very personal one. Your concern about your perfection has that about it which calls for your prayerful consideration. This is especially true in time of retreat. Indeed, you need silence to listen to Christ. Scripture reminds you that God is not in the whirlwind. Even in retreat you can be distracted by otherwise good thoughts which then, however, do not give the Holy Spirit a great deal of opportunity to operate in your soul. It is a very false concept of prayer that would call for constant talking on your part. Indeed, you do not have to be saying something to God all the time. Prayer is two-way communication. In your prayer do more listening. Give God a chance to speak to you.

Fr. Evoy: So often, when you carefully observe two people engaged in conversation, you will witness what the French call the "dialogue of the deaf." Neither is really listening to the other.

Each is waiting for the other to stop, so that she can get in her say. There is a kind of half-hearing going on, but no real listening. It reminds one somewhat of the training given students in debate. They are taught to attend closely to what their opponents are saying solely in order to find flaws in their case and refute it, but never really to listen.

I wonder if you might not do something like that with God? Is it not possible to keep so busy talking with people, or even to him, that you never really listen to the Holy Spirit? But how do you know that the Holy Spirit is going to talk to you? Because our Lord told you so. When speaking of the Paraclete, he said, "All things whatsoever I have told him, he will make clear to you." The Holy Spirit, himself, loves you and wants to communicate with you. Even though you may not know the best way to listen to him, you can be certain that if you are talking in nonstop fashion to others the Holy Spirit is not easily going to find the opportunity to speak to you.

Fr. Christoph: This, we are told, is the day of the dialogue and not of the monologue. You cannot very well carry on this type of supremely important listening in your prayer if you spend your time in distracting conversation. On the other hand, to be trying to think about God continually, with no communication with other people, may be productive of fatigue rather than spiritual benefit to you.

Fr. Evoy: A further word about the Holy Spirit's communicating with you. How does he speak to you? As a matter of fact, you do not have to be really concerned how the Holy Spirit will manage to speak to you. Presumably you remain open to the Holy Spirit, and because he is desirous of communicating with you he will find a way. It is rather disconcerting, however, to reflect that you could make his communicating with one of your sisters very difficult by endlessly chatting with her. It is highly unlikely that the

Holy Spirit will compete with your small talk for sister's attention. This, then, is one place where real charity toward your sister would call for some reasonable silence on your part, so that the Spirit of Love can get an "in." Dialogue can be a most beneficial encounter. You certainly would not knowingly exclude the Holy Spirit, who is infinite love, from communicating with the one he loves.

Fr. Christoph: And this communicating with the Holy Spirit need not call for many words on a sister's part. Even between human beings there is wordless communication. On occasion you may be with your family, but you do not feel the need to be engaged in conversation with them. You enjoy, likewise, being with your community but you do not feel that you should be always talking or even listening. You simply want to be there. Indeed, there is such a thing as a comfortable and expressive silence. Father Evoy and I will be sitting next to each other on the same plane, not saying a word. Nevertheless, we enjoy the company of each other. It is the same in your relationship with the Holy Spirit. God can make his presence felt without a word being said.

Fr. Evoy: In the Palm Sunday accounts of both Matthew and Luke there is another point. Our Lord instructs the Apostles to bring him the ass and her foal. He goes on to say that if anyone inquires why they are doing so, they should answer, "Because the Lord has need of them." Christ could rightly have said, "Tell them that their owner wants them." God, as their creator, is their only complete and perfect owner. And yet, notice the considerateness of the God-man. He instructs the Apostles to give an explanation to those inquiring so that they might freely permit the animals to be taken away.

God is also man's owner; indeed, man's only owner. Nevertheless, he does not exercise his absolute dominion in a way that disregards, let alone violates, human freedom. Not even after your religious profession does he exercise his absolute dominion over you without regard for your freedom. Instead, in his tremendous respect for you, he awaits your leave, your permission. He does not coerce your obedience. He does not demand your love. Strange as it may seem, in a sense, God stands "hat in hand," hopefully awaiting your "yes" to him.

While your vows give you a special intimacy with God, they bring with it special obligations. Because God wants a free service, and not a groveling, obsequious cooperation, he presents religious life to you, not by way of command but as a counsel of perfection. This means that you did not have to embrace the religious state. Indeed, you would not necessarily have been less good had you ignored this precious invitation. But once you have accepted the call of Christ, you have put yourself in a special relationship to him.

This raises a very interesting consideration relative to vocation. God does not force anyone into religious life. You do not serve God in religious life because you *have* to. It is true he needs you. But he gives you an invitation to work with him. There is no forcing. The idea of *having to* follow Christ in religious life could mean being burdened with the *necessity to*. And this is not what Christ wants of you. He wants you to be joyful in the Lord. He wants you to serve him in your religious vocation because you love him and not because of a threatened "or else." Yours is a tremendously free gift to God. And giving to him out of love has the power to make it a source of true joy.

Notwithstanding such complete freedom in your vocation, the recognition of God's absolute ownership throws much light on your life as a religious. With the taking of your religious vows, you promised to strive to exercise your custodianship in a special way. Your life under vows is first, your willing recognition of the absolute dominion God has over you, and second, your free gift of self back to him as completely as possible. It means you have used your God-given freedom to give God your greatest gift, the immediate and irrevocable surrender of yourself, in love, to your Creator. Now you do not want to do anything unbecoming a religious, because you hold as precious all you have vowed to him.

It is well to reflect on the manner in which this complete and immediate gift of yourself is accomplished through your vows. Under poverty you have renounced to God every material thing you could have possessed in the world, including a home of your own, which could have meant so much to you as a woman. Also in this offering were all the prized possessions which women are wont to safeguard over the years. Under your vow of chastity, you have given up, for the love of God, the lifelong companionship of a husband, with the kind of outlet this would have provided for your love and affection, as well as the children that might have been born of this love. And finally, under your third vow you have completed the emptying of yourself by freely surrendering to him, for life, areas of licit independence. What is left? In pronouncing your vows, you equivalently have said to God, "Under these three vows, I return to you all of me." From this time forward each of you should be able to say with St. Paul, "I live, now, not I, but Christ lives in me."

Fr. Christoph: The perfection of your surrender is found in the vow of obedience. If you did not have a very great love of God and did not trust that in his divine goodness your obedience would not be taken advantage of by superiors, you could not so courageously pronounce that vow which makes you so vulnerable. I cannot think of a better word than vulnerability to express the faith implied in obedience. Sisters, you expose yourselves so much when you place yourselves completely at the disposition of another person.

Fr. Evoy: This is a very real exposure. Your vow of obedience completes the total gift of yourself to God in love. In your vow of obedience you leave yourself open to deep hurt. To assume that God could never permit such hurt would be unrealistic. Mature religious men and women have been deeply hurt within the framework of this vow. Hence this exposure, under your vow of obedience, is no make believe. Even your presumed good will in superiors does not lessen your vulnerability. Through this vow you put your life completely in God's hands.

Our Lord himself said, "Greater love than this no man has that he lay down his life for his friend." Indeed, if there is a greater act of love for God than the full living out of your vows, I do not know what it is. No wonder that your life is misunderstood by some people. To them, it is incomprehensible. It appears to be a dehumanizing and depersonalizing thing. It appears to surrender too much that is human. But love is that way. It does not count the cost. It does not reserve anything for self. Every great love elicits from the lover a surrender that is complete, and this is what you have given to God through your vows.

Fr. Christoph: But in pledging one's vows to God there is another side to the picture. The need that God has for his creatures in this Gospel episode is magnified indefinitely when you consider his need of you for the development and expansion of the kingdom of God on earth. Christ tells the Apostles that he has need of his creatures. More, Christ has need of you. In the words of St. Paul, you become God's coadjutors.

Fr. Evoy: God did not have to work out the development of his kingdom this way. But according to the operation of his divine economy in salvation history, he needs you. God, who "so loved the world as to give his only-begotten son," wants men, women, and children to know of his love for each of them. But love is not an abstract thing. Man knows love in a meaningful way only through the experience of loving and being loved. A human being knows divine love as a meaningful reality solely through experiencing human love.

So God depends on you and me to show people the reality of his love for them. Father Christoph and I by loving someone can show that person what a man's genuine love is. The warmth of a woman's love we cannot show. Christ depends on you for that. If one is loved with the true love of a man only, that person knows but one-half of the human expression of divine love; he can know the experience of being loved by a woman only through you. Because you are recognizably God's, when you show someone a real, personal, *pure* love you need few words to support your assertion that God loves him. If you love, to the best of your ability, those whom you encounter, God will take care that your best gift of love will not be given in vain.

Fr. Christoph: Sisters, there is another observation we may make about the triumphant entry of Christ into Jerusalem on Palm Sunday. On that day, the multitude cried out, "Hosannah to the Son of David." Less than a week later a similar crowd would cry out, "Away with him! Crucify him!" It may happen that the praise you receive today will turn into scorn tomorrow. Even in religious life this is a possibility.

Fr. Evoy: In fact, it seems highly probable that many persons who on Palm Sunday cried out, "Hosannah!" less than a week later also screamed, "Crucify him!" Unfortunately, these people were fickle. They may have, later on, been sorry for what they had done on Good Friday.

Sisters, an occupational hazard of a person who risks loving others is this human fickleness. Those who will be loyal to you with constancy are not too numerous. One or more seemingly very close to you can prove to be false. To love others, to really let yourself care for them is sometimes to court hurt. Is your striving to love and care for them worth that risk? Does not our Lord answer this question for you? He knew well that some of those enthusiastically shouting, "Hosannah!" would later cry, "Crucify him!" Yet he cared about those people. He loved them. And he wants all his faithful followers, despite the risks involved, to care about and to love people.

Experience testifies to the fact that those who really love people seem to have the greatest share of peace and happiness in this world.

17 Christ's Last Discourse

Fr. Christoph: We have been speaking of the need that God has of you, a need conditioned obviously by his will to save men through men. The purpose of your daily reflection and prayer is, in part, to strengthen and deepen your commitment to God. As a result of your past reflections you have doubtlessly been moved to some positive action that will help you serve Christ more faithfully. Reflecting on Christ's last discourse should help to strengthen and confirm you in your good resolutions.

We are going to touch upon the very heart of the most beautiful romance of time and eternity, a love story that never began and that will never end. It is a love story that never began because from all eternity God has loved you. It is a love story that will never end because he will love you throughout the endless reaches of eternity. The climax of this love story in time, for Christ, will be the sacrifice of his life for all mankind—for you and for me especially. The events that you will reflect on are not to be regarded as merely historical. Each one must realize the *for-me-ness* of the Passion of Christ. It makes no difference that others share in the benefits of Redemption. You are the beneficiary of God as well as his debtor, for Christ died for you.

I suggest that you read and meditate on Chapters 13–17 of the

Gospel of St. John. Here Jesus speaks with a simplicity and sincerity no one can miss. And it is John, the beloved disciple, who has preserved our Lord's words in the setting of the Last Supper. In the events in that upper room and in his discourse to his Apostles and his prayer for them, Christ's burning love for his Heavenly Father and for you and me is poured out. From the wealth of thoughts found in St. John's account of the last discourse of Christ before his Passion, I should like to touch upon a few points.

> Before the feast of the passover, Jesus, knowing that the hour had come for him to pass out of this world to the Father, having loved his own who were in the world, loved them to the end. (John 13:1.)

Strive to capture the depth of meaning in those words. Do they not help you appreciate the love of God a little more? Christ, with his divine foreknowledge, knew that his Apostles before the morrow would abandon him. Peter, to whom he would entrust his Church, would commit the worst sin, outside of deicide— namely, swearing with an oath that he did not even know Christ.

Yet, despite their shortcomings Christ loved them. He knew their weaknesses, their ambition, their fears, their cowardice. He understood them, and that is the key to his love for them.

Sisters, Christ loves you as you are. If you are almost wearied from hearing these words, they are repeated only because this love of God for you *as you are* is a fact to be reckoned with, especially in religious life. And in turn, you may need to remind yourselves that you are not creators nor renovators of people. You cannot fashion them with chisel and mallet so as to make them to your own image and likeness. You, too, are to love them as they are.

The Gospel account continues:

Now after he had washed their feet and put on his gar-
ments, when he had reclined again, he said to them, "Do
you know what I have done to you? You call me Master and
Lord, and you say well, for so I am. If, therefore, I the Lord
and Master have washed your feet, you also ought to wash
the feet of one another. For I have given you an example,
that as I have done to you, so you also should do. Amen,
Amen, I say to you, no servant is greater than his master.
. . . (John 13:12–16.)

"As I have done to you, so you also should do." Throughout
his life Christ gives us an example, but it is seldom that he takes
time out to remind us of this. Elsewhere he said, "Who follows
me walks not in darkness" and "learn of me," but this is the
only place where he, in a sense, spells out what the following of
him really means. Christ reminded his Apostles that he was their
Lord and Master, and then he went on to humble himself before
them by performing the task of a servant. Our Lord came among
men as one who serves. By his action, he shows us that true
nobility is not so much a matter of position as it is of disposition.
The Apostles needed this lesson because they were even then
discussing their place in Christ's kingdom.

And you may need the lesson. There must be in you a willingness to accept any role given you in the community. Even those
in authority must be humble and ready to take on insignificant
tasks. Moreover, all cannot be leaders. Besides those who direct,
there must be those who carry out the directives. And no one
should feel that even the most menial task is unimportant when
it is done for the love of God. By his behavior, Christ rules out
envy and disordered ambition.

"I have given you an example, that as I have done to you, so
you also should do." Here, our Lord is saying, in effect, "Serve
me in your neighbor. I will not be physically present, as I am
now, before you much longer. You will, however, have my breth-

ren, and as long as you have done it unto one of these, I will
consider it as having been done to me." Christ gives divine approval to serving him in any way possible. Often enough you may
choose the way in which you will serve Christ; often the manner,
because you are religious, will be chosen for you. It may even
be that when the manner is chosen for you, what you do may be
more pleasing to Christ and more meritorious.

Later on, Christ interrupts his thoughts and turns to his followers at table and remarks, "Amen, amen, I say to you, one of
you will betray me." And in surprise, each one asks, "Is it I,
Lord?" There is a sincerity in this inquiry which may easily be
overlooked. The Apostles were not sure how they would act
when circumstances would be challenging and demanding. St.
Paul, too, had this fear for himself, and he reminds us, "Let him
who thinks he stands take heed lest he fall."

You do not know with certainty what you will do in the
presence of an unusually attractive temptation. But this should
only serve to make you cautious and prayerful, not fearful.
Please God, at this moment you have the confidence that you
will not betray him who is indeed your changeless friend. However, one Apostle did betray him. From Judas we learn the lesson
of eternal vigilance. Judas allowed an inordinate desire to rule
and so ruined his life. He was not watchful nor careful. Again
St. Paul reminds us, "I chastise my body and bring it under subjection, lest after having preached the gospel to others, I, myself,
become a castaway." This is a reminder that anyone can fall and
that it is not religious life which will save you but the manner
in which you live your religious life.

As the Gospel account continues, Philip asks Christ, "Lord,
show us the Father and it is enough for us." Jesus said to him,
"Have I been so long a time with you, and you have not known
me?" Some of you have been in religious life one year, ten years,
maybe thirty or more years, and I wonder if Christ can chide you
in the same fashion. Through your years of studying and your

following of our Lord you should have grown in your knowledge of him. Recall what Father Evoy said to you about demanding or at least expecting God to measure up to your conceptions of the divine. You have so little knowledge of how God works. "Have I been so long a time with you?" he says. And how long has he been with you?

Christ makes himself present to you through so many persons —through your religious companions, through the children whom you teach, the aged for whom you care, the merchants with whom you come in contact. Indeed, through all the people who come into your lives our Lord makes himself present. For each one is, in a true sense, Christ. If you saw your neighbor as Christ, you would not only treat him more graciously, but you also would lead him more effectively to God.

Twice during the discourse at the Last Supper Christ calls upon his Apostles to keep the commandment of love. "This is my commandment, that you love one another as I have loved you." And again, "A new commandment I give you, that you love one another." How Christ has loved us! The Incarnation only makes sense on the supposition that man is loveable enough that God should want to redeem him. This is why you need never question the loveableness of those whom you are commanded to love.

There are two points to remember here. The first is that you are to love *one another.* You leave no one out of your love. The second point is that you are to love them *as Christ loves them.* Indeed, Christ goes on to say that in this way will all men know that you are his, because you have this love for your fellowmen. If there is any virtue for which Christians and especially religious should be noted, it is love. This was such an outstanding characteristic of the early Christians that the pagans were wont to say in admiration, "Behold how they love one another."

This love has the power to unite; "that all may know that you are *mine.*" Indeed, in the midst of his exhortation to love, Christ lifts his voice up to his Heavenly Father and says, "I pray . . . that all may be one, even as thou, Father, in me and I in thee; that they also may be one in us." And he would make this manifestation of love a proof to all mankind of his divine mission, for Christ adds, "that the world may believe that thou has sent me." Our Lord is asking that the Apostles be true witnesses to his divinity and to his Church. That same Christ is asking you to be so united in charity that all may recognize you as his very own and accept him as you do.

18 *Agony in the Garden*

Fr. Evoy: The following is the brief account of the happenings in the Garden of Gethsemane according to St. John:

> After saying these things, Jesus went forth with his disciples beyond the torrent of Cedron, where there was a garden into which he and his disciples entered. Now Judas, who betrayed him, also knew the place, since Jesus had often met there together with his disciples. Judas, then, taking the cohort, and attendants from the chief priests and Pharisees, came there with lanterns, and torches, and weapons.
>
> Jesus therefore knowing all that was to come upon him, went forth and said to them, "Whom do you seek?" They answered him, "Jesus of Nazareth." Jesus said to them, "I am he." Now Judas, who betrayed him, was also standing with them. When, therefore, he said to them, "I am he," they drew back and fell to the ground. So he asked them again, "Whom do you seek?" And they said, Jesus of Nazareth." Jesus answered, "I have told you that I am he. If, therefore, you seek me, let these go their way." That the word which he said might be fulfilled, "Of those whom thou hast given me, I have not lost one." (John 18:1–9.)

Fr. Christoph: The human mind cannot discover an adequate explanation of the problem of pain. We are disturbed by the suffering that finds its way into the lives of the good—those who are trying, those who are trusting, those who are serving God to the best of their abilities. Looking at all this from a merely human point of view, it would seem that these people deserve better treatment from the hand of God. It is so hard for us to reconcile the goodness of God on the one hand and the incidence of pain on the other. We can, of course, fall back on Scripture and in the context of our faith, which proclaims the goodness of God, conclude with St. Paul that "to them that love God all things work together unto good." We can also say that suffering, when borne patiently, can be acceptable expiation for sin and merit God's grace. But there is so much misery, so much pain, so much suffering that the antinomy remains—how do we reconcile the mercy and goodness of God with the suffering in this world?

No life is free from suffering. Indeed, some seem to have more than their share of it. But, it is against the background of Christ's passion that suffering becomes intelligible. You can offer it up to God in atonement for your own sins. You can use it as reparation to God for the sins of others. You can, likewise, use it as a help to a fitting detachment from the pleasurable things of life. Indeed, suffering can become the proof of your love for Christ who said, "If anyone wishes to come after me, let him deny himself, and take up his cross daily, and follow me."

It would be wrong to hold that the life of man should be one perpetual, painful experience. However, since painful experiences enter into your lives, you ought to fit them into the pattern of salvation and sanctification. Since you want to be like Christ, you ought to accept the sufferings that come into your life, not fatalistically, but willingly. To imitate Christ ever more closely, all other things being equal, you desire suffering, because Christ chose to suffer to show his love for you. In this manner you show your love for him.

Many of the saints looked upon suffering this way. St. Theresa of Avila prayed to God, "Either let me suffer or let me die," and St. Mary Magdalen of Pazzi prayed, "Do not let me die; let me suffer." People like these are not masochistic. They do not love suffering for the sake of suffering. But in it they see an opportunity to identify themselves more with Christ, thereby giving to the world a lesson it stands sadly in need of, that in order to "fill up what is wanting of the sufferings of Christ," as St. Paul says of himself, man must at some times suffer.

Fr. Evoy: I think we should frankly acknowledge our dissatisfaction with the adequacy of every explanation of suffering which has been given us. Moreover, it is realistic to recognize that, this side of the grave, we never will be given a fully satisfying account of it. Nevertheless, it is of some substantial help in accepting the unquestionable fact of suffering to recall that an all-loving, all-powerful God permits it. But this only furnishes us with a basis for an acceptance of suffering, not with an explanation of it. The understanding of human suffering is so difficult because suffering in itself is an evil. For man, evil remains a mystery, ultimately resolvable only within the mystery of Christ.

Fr. Christoph: Despite its mystery, suffering fits into the divine plan. In the long history of man's existence on earth there have been sufferings caused by such physical phenomena as illness, earthquakes, hurricanes, and famine. There have been sufferings too caused by the meanness, cruelty, thoughtlessness, and inconsiderateness of others. All these sufferings call for some kind of explanation. But to understand perfectly these evils requires a canvas as broad as history itself and a time perspective as long as eternity—which only God has. What I am saying is that God alone can give us the complete answer to the problem of suffering.

Fr. Evoy: Despite the fact that suffering remains for us such a mystery, we nevertheless have some knowledge about it. We learn from the Passion that there can be a very close link between suffering and love. Christ did not have to suffer. He did not have to shed even one drop of his blood in order to redeem us. Once he had inserted himself into the human race and had become man "like unto us in all things, sin alone excepted," he thereby became *the* man speaking in our behalf to the transcendent God. He was indeed both the Son of Man and the Son of God and so his every action was of infinite worth to man.

All that was needed was for Christ to ask his eternal Father to pardon the sins of man. Such a request by a divine person who was a man would have merited divine pardon for all men. It would have sufficed, then, had Christ merely asked his Father for the forgiveness and restoration of man. Why then the Passion? Because the Father loved us, he willed his son to suffer. God knows that a human being needs tangible evidence that he is loved. It was his Father's will that Christ should give us an unquestionable proof of God's love for man. And Christ's suffering constituted just such evidence. This is the reason the Father gave his only-begotten Son.

Fr. Christoph: Indeed, St. John reminds us that "God so loved the world that he gave his only-begotten Son." The Passion our Lord underwent shows us the length to which his love would carry him. Shortly before his Passion Christ told his Apostles, "I must go up to Jerusalem to suffer many things." Months before, he said to the multitude, "I am the Good Shepherd." The Good Shepherd lays down his life for us. Surely this is love proved to the limit.

You have heard Father Evoy say that love and suffering sometimes go hand in hand. I would go further and say that there is never any great love here on earth which does not involve some kind of pain one time or another. Thus, suffering for the sake of the beloved becomes a test and proof of one's love.

Fr. Evoy: A person who loves another is willing to do what is exceedingly painful for the sake of that person. The willingness to suffer, however, is not in itself a proof of love. Unfortunately there can be such a thing as wasted suffering. And suffering that has no connection whatever with love certainly appears to be wasted. Even suffering merely in passive submission to the will of God is partially wasted, inasmuch as it fails to be the expression of one's love for God that it could and should be. Suffering gives its maximum enrichment to a person's life only when its acceptance is an expression of love. Not one iota of the suffering Christ experienced throughout his Passion was wasted.

The suffering of his Passion trumpeted forth two facts. First, as we have already indicated, it bespoke the love of the Eternal Father and of the God-man for you. From the human point of view it was a most fitting medium for the expression of his love, for it is one you readily understand. God speaks to us in a manner befitting our human nature. The suffering of Christ thus became the medium eloquently proclaiming God's love for us. In contemplating the Passion we begin to understand our Lord's words, "Greater love than this no man has that he lay down his life for his friend."

Secondly, Christ's suffering unmistakably spelled out for us the reality of sin. The priest, at Mass, testifies to this when he says, "This is the chalice of my blood which for you and for many is poured forth unto the remission of sins." Our Lord left us in no doubt that his blood was shed for the removal of sins. Indeed, not to see that Christ's suffering proclaimed both the facts of God's love and of man's sins is to fail to view the Passion in proper perspective.

Fr. Christoph: Over and above this evidence of the fact of sin, the Passion of Christ gives us an idea of the heinousness of sin. God does not want us to have any illusions about sin. He wants to impress upon us all how terrible an affront sin is to him. We have considered the consequences of sin and the fact that sin, of itself, deserves hell. Now we are looking at another consequence of sin, namely, that it called for the sacrifice of Jesus Christ.

Fr. Evoy: Suffering for the sake of suffering can be idolatry. In and of itself suffering is not a sacred thing. Yet, because of its role in the redemption of man, suffering has been elevated and given a new meaning. Our redemption was purchased for us through very painful suffering. That redemption is to be applied and thus carried on through suffering. While Christ purchased that redemption through great suffering in his human nature, the contemporary, gloriously resurrected Christ is unable through suffering in his own human nature to apply this redemption. He suffers, therefore, in his Mystical Body. Because you are members of the Whole Christ, he can still suffer in you. Wasted suffering is so tragic because suffering can have such a tremendous redemptive value. Indeed, suffering may be converted into sacrifice—that is to say, into an action made sacred by being offered to God.

Sisters, within the framework of sacrifice, you should remind yourselves that by reason of your religious life, you stand at the threshold of the mystery of all the apparently wasted in this world. By what you are, you constitute a case for so many things which have been left unfulfilled. All the potentials which were yours for wifehood and physical motherhood have been offered to God. In thus being sacrificed they have been given a redemptive value.

Fr. Christoph: By your dedicated life you are telling the world that many apparently wasted things make sense. You are not surprised if a large segment of the world regards you as foolish, since to them sacrifice is only a painful experience which does not make sense. Isaias, foretelling the Passion of Christ, throws some light on Christ's sorrow, when he says, "What utility is there in my blood?"

Father Evoy reminded you that even our Lord could be hurt deeply only by those whom he loved. And the behavior of some of those who were so close to him during his public life and whom he loved would be a source of deep sorrow. In his agony he foresaw that Judas would betray him, Peter deny him, and his Apostles, save one, would abandon him. Very few of his close friends would be standing at the foot of his cross to comfort him. No wonder the psalmist puts these words into the mouth of Christ, "I looked for one to comfort me and there was none!"

Fr. Evoy: Isaias says, in effect, that our Lord's human experience was "What is the point, what is the use of all this suffering?" Christ appears to have had the experience of futility. He foresaw that some upon whom he depended would let him down. In his human nature Christ must have been very discouraged. The anticipation of futility in one's strivings is always disheartening, and our Lord gives us no reason to believe that he was not so affected as he foresaw the disappointing behavior of his friends. It is so easy for us to lose sight of Christ the man in our preoccupation with his being God. We need to remind ourselves that he is very human. Psalm 21, which describes the Passion in detail, reassures us that our Lord knows what discouragement is, because he was discouraged. He appreciates what it means to be abandoned by friends, because he himself was abandoned by friends. He understands *exactly* how hurt we can be because he himself has been through it.

Fr. Christoph: I may add that the futility of Christ's sufferings is accentuated when we consider it in relation to all mankind. They are his by creation and by inheritance. He will purchase them with his blood shed on Calvary, and yet there will be those who will not accept him. But the thought of this did not stop

Christ. He was to suffer in such a way and to such an extent that the salvation of all mankind would be possible. Yet he knew that all would not be saved. And this knowledge contributed to his becoming sorrowful unto death.

Fr. Evoy: When we contemplate the torture of Christ evident in the sweat of blood, we wonder what caused such excruciating suffering. No one of us feels that he has the complete answer to this question. We can surmise, I believe, at least part of the answer. To begin with, since Christ was a psychologically healthy man, he would naturally find the anticipation of a most painful and shameful death a very abhorrent prospect. His human nature, therefore, would cringe in the face of his approaching Passion.

It is well for us to recall at this time that Christ did not yet know experientially in his own human nature what death was. For our Lord, there was still the not-yet-experienced element in his knowledge of death. As we study Christ in the Gospels, we continue to be impressed with the fact that the God-man is so very human, "like unto us in all things, sin excepted."

In our attempt to understand Christ's sufferings one reflection, I think, is of utmost importance. It needs to be repeated that while a person can be hurt by many people, his close friends alone are capable of hurting him most deeply. Indeed, only those we truly love or want to love can hurt us in this way. Christ was hurt in this way. His heart was broken.

Fr. Christoph: "And falling into an agony he prayed the more earnestly." We become so easily discouraged in our prayer. We so often tend to give up praying when our prayers are not immediately answered. Christ teaches us how to pray. We are reminded by Luke that Christ prayed the selfsame prayer, "Father, if thou art willing, remove this cup from me." So often we find even religious complaining that their prayers are not heard.

Nothing could be farther from the truth. Indeed, even the prayer of the hardened sinner is heard.

When you pray you should pray as Christ did, ". . . yet not my will but thine be done." You submit your will to God in the knowledge that he knows what is best for you. Christ instructed you, "ask the Father anything in my name and he will give it to you." So you ask. When you do not receive, you feel let down by God. So often you pray for what you *want*. You always get what you *need*.

What you want may be contrary to your good, and since you have submitted your will to God, in his merciful goodness he does not grant what you have prayed for. You resent this. But should you? May it not be that the health you asked for would not be for your ultimate benefit; that the success you wanted would be a source of pride? Let me repeat, you get what you need, and although you are encouraged to pray for what you want, you do not always know what is good for you. You submit your will to the divine will and you have enough faith and trust in God that his will is always the best for you.

Fr. Evoy: When you analyze it, what was Christ's prayer in the garden? What was he saying to his Father? Was he not pleading, "Please, Father, help me," when he asked his Father to let the chalice pass from him? And even in his agony, Christ still gives you the prototype of all prayer, for after making his request, he adds, "yet not my will but thine be done." Here is the very human Christ who, though steeped in extreme suffering, still gives you a model for your prayer. The perfect prayer always ends "but not my will but thine be done."

Fr. Christoph: Another reflection comes to mind as we contemplate the agony of Christ. The Apostles, so recently refreshed by their first Holy Communion, would fail Christ. Peter, John and James had, in addition, the memory of the Transfiguration to strengthen them, and yet how disappointing their conduct, especially Peter's. Christ, no stranger to human weakness, understood. He would forgive the weakness in his Apostles. You receive our Lord, perhaps daily in Holy Communion and ought to be saints because of your intimate association with him. Yet, so often, you feel anything but saintly. The temptation is to be discouraged by your apparent lack of progress. You can take some comfort from the behavior of those who were with Christ at the Last Supper. And as Christ did not reject his Apostles, neither will he reject you.

Fr. Evoy: It might be well to conclude our contemplation of the Agony in the Garden with a few final reflections. Perhaps nowhere else in Christ's visible life on earth did he manifest more strikingly both the depth of his humanness and the magnificence of his personality. Did we not see him as very human, we might be tempted to question our ability to follow him. And as we glimpse the greatness of his Person, we are moved spontaneously to awe and admiration. Once we see him as the inexpressibly magnificent but still very human Christ, we know that we can love him with an intense personal love which does not count the cost of the service we give him.

19 *Christ Before the High Priest and Pilate*

Fr. Christoph: You have often reflected upon your own spiritual state, and anxious to improve it you have realized that there are defects you must rid yourself of and virtues you must strengthen. The Passion of Christ becomes a motive for carrying out your good intentions.

You juxtapose your own life—your own aspirations, your willingness to suffer and to suppress those tendencies which are less good—to what Christ has done for you. You see that what you have been doing, are doing, and propose to do for him is small in comparison. Reflection on the Passion should fill you with even greater determination and generosity to live for Christ. Indeed, the desire to live your religious life as well as you can with the help of God's grace seems a rather small response in return to Christ for all that he has done for you.

We now come to Christ's arrest in the Garden. A host of events took place between the midnight arrest of Christ and his crucifixion. He was brought before Annas and Caiphas and lastly before Pilate, and before each of them numerous accusations were made against him.

Fr. Evoy: As we accompany Christ from the Garden, we come first to the house of Annas. It would appear that they stopped for the visit at this house for two reasons; first, very likely the Sanhedrin was not yet ready for the mockery of the so-called trial, so badly needed time would be gained by this stalling tactic; secondly, this was a convenient way of throwing a token of recognition to Annas. Annas, the father-in-law of Caiphas, the high priest, had himself formerly been the high priest. Thus, to bring Christ to Annas was politically a shrewd move.

Annas asked Christ to tell him about his disciples and his doctrine. Not one word did the loyal Christ say about his disciples. He proceeded immediately to talk about his doctrine. At this point, a member of the household of Annas, in order to curry favor with his employer, stepped forth and struck our Lord in the face. Christ immediately challenged him, "If I have done wrong, say it; if not, why do you strike me?" Our Lord is saying, in effect, that a person may never be used.

We need to be reminded frequently that one may not use a human being for any reason. Even for the most wonderful work conceivable, it is not permissible to use another person. A man is never expendable by one of his fellowmen. Even though the good of the religious community or the good of the Church would seem to require, for example, that a sister or even a child in school be treated unjustly, such may not be done. Regardless of the situation, the reputation, dignity, or even the health of another person may not be sacrificed for the common good. This reminds me of Father Christoph's remark earlier about the tremendous vulnerability inherent in the vow of obedience. Unfortunately, it must be faced that under obedience a person can be, and more than one has been, used.

It must be understood that every sister and every other person whom we encounter is possessed of an essential, inviolable, intrinsic dignity and therefore may never on any account be used as if she were a thing. A human being may not be treated as a thing even for the sake of the kingdom of God, let alone in order to secure peace or to meet the demands of some important person.

I would not even think of using a sister, because of my genuine love for her. I can never permit one I love to be used regardless of any other consideration. If I am in a position of authority, I hope that I will always remember our Lord's protective considerateness for his own in the Garden, expressed openly in the words "Let these go their way."

We come next to the farcical legal trial in which witnesses brought false charges against Christ. Our Lord taught a valuable lesson here. He let these lying witnesses talk on without interruption. There was no need to refute them. And there, in the midst of the Sanhedrin, Caiphas was intelligent enough to see that soon it would be apparent to all that the witnesses were lying. Sooner or later liars betray that they are lying. Is it not strange how ready we are to rise to our own defense in the face of lies about ourselves? Reflection will show that you often have no obligation to go to your own defense when you are being unfairly or unjustly attacked. You are *not* free, however, to stand idly by when one you love is being lied about or otherwise unjustly or unfairly treated.

Fr. Christoph: Christ was the victim of calumny. If he had tried to defend himself against his enemies, his defense would have been misinterpreted. His silence gave eloquent testimony of his meekness. Long before, he had said, "Learn of me who am meek," and now he gives an example of meekness. Christ is telling you that you may remain silent when you are unjustly or unfairly treated. Indeed, your protestations of innocence in the face of calumny may seem shallow and inadequate. Unless the reputation of the Church, of your congregation, or of someone else is at stake you seldom find it necessary to make a defense. However, when someone calumniates a superior or anyone else, you should come to her defense. There is an *esprit de corps,* a love of neighbor, that dictates this.

Fr. Evoy: When you are hurt, you may, out of fear, take it and say nothing. To do so, however, is weakness and not virtue. But if you can ascertain that you are the only one being hurt, then you may choose to do nothing about it because you want more closely to resemble Christ. In this case, it would be not weakness but meekness. On the other hand, you could never condone unfair treatment of another.

In this travesty of justice Christ was actually prejudged. The evidence was arranged and presented in an effort to make him look guilty. He had been sentenced to death before he ever walked into that trial. The only task of his judges was to find legal grounds for their action. Their purpose was not to prove that he was actually guilty—which would be impossible—but solely to go through the legal motions of a trial. True justice itself was the last thing they wanted. But they needed the trappings of justice in order to officially sentence him to death. Without this facade of justice they would not have achieved their end. Their purpose was to get rid of him. Whether he was innocent was beside the point. In fact, it was not even an academic consideration. He had to be destroyed. Nothing else mattered.

In all candor, one does not live long in religious life before realizing that a religious can experience something resembling what Christ experienced here. She can be tried and sentenced before she has a hearing. In fact, there might be very little point in her trying to defend herself. But Christ is still her model in this unfair treatment. He knows from his own experience what it means to be unjustly condemned. It would have been useless to try to defend himself in his trial, even if he had chosen to do so. His judges would not have listened. Their minds were closed.

Fr. Christoph: Father Evoy remarked that people can be misjudged even in religious life. Since I view reality through my own eyes, there is the human tendency to protect my ego. There is the possibility that I will not see what is there. Blinded by passion or the need to save myself, my vision might well be selective. Hence I could misjudge another on the basis of my own needs. Most religious communities can chronicle the lives of individuals who have been unjustly accused by superiors, fellow religious, or by others. Not even the founders of religious communities have been exempt from this kind of treatment.

We can, for example, recall St. Alphonsus, founder of the Congregation of the Most Holy Redeemer, and Father Moreau, founder of the Congregation of Holy Cross, both of whom were forced to live outside their communities, and Father Hecker, the founder of the Congregation of St. Paul, whose apostolate and writings suffered from the interpretation of men, zealous for the faith. All these were victims of calumny. Time has vindicated these men, but in their lifetime they certainly suffered. In the acceptance of their sufferings they stand out in the history of the Church. Christ was their model. Each of these men was familiar with our Lord's words, "The servant is not greater than his master." "If they have done these things to me they will also do them to you." The acceptance of such treatment is the stuff from which saints are made.

Fr. Evoy: Father Christoph, speaking of how our Lord was viewed, used the word "misunderstood." But Christ was not misunderstood by Caiphas. On the contrary, Caiphas understood only too well. He and some of his colleagues were playing a game of make believe. Christ had to die. It was as cold-blooded as that. It is likely, however, that Christ was misunderstood by some of his persecutors. I wonder which of these two groups Christ found the more difficult to deal with. I have a suspicion that those operating with malice were not as difficult for him to

cope with as were the other well-meaning, misunderstanding persecutors. How was Christ to act towards those who really believed,
as they had so often been told, that this Jesus was dangerous, a
threat to their entire cultural heritage and to the welfare of the
Jewish people and thus deserving of death? Is there anything
harder to bear than people who say they mean well?

Someone has remarked, "Give me a choice and I'll take malice
in preference to profound ignorance in my opponents every
time." So often, when religious have been treated unjustly the
presumption is that it has been by persons who meant well but
who misunderstood. Father Teilhard de Chardin is regarded as a
great man today. You are all aware that he suffered at the hands
of others. Was he dealt with from malice? We do not know that
he was. He does appear to have been misunderstood. A number
of persons, including some of his superiors, questioned his ortho-
doxy. Christlike, he submitted in obedience to those who said
they could not acquiesce. And I would suspect, since he was a
very sensitive person, that this hurt him deeply.

We would like to think that those who were keeping de
Chardin off at a comfortable distance, were doing so in good
faith. They seem to have misunderstood him and what he was
endeavoring to say. Recall what I just said about how difficult
it is to deal with certain persons who seem to misunderstand.

I cannot possibly square with my conscience dealing severely
with a really well-meaning person no matter how hurtful he is.
But people who seem to be lacking understanding and say they
are really desirous of being helpful can be very burdensome. I
can at times make something of a case for reprisals against one
who appears to be malicious. I might, for instance, feel that this
person needs to be taught a lesson. At any rate, the malicious
person really asked for it. But it is more difficult to justify re-
taliation against one who says he means well. I think dealing
with him often is so frustrating, we spontaneously look for evidence of malice. Clear-cut malice is so much easier to cope with.

May God spare us from those who keep telling us they mean well.

Fr. Christoph: Religious are capable of hurting their companions in so many ways. Words, actions, and even silence—these can be so wounding. Occasionally, the religious who is unable to get a hearing for his problems or constructive ideas experiences overwhelming futility. There are two unhealthy reactions to being misunderstood. One of the unhealthy reactions to being misunderstood is to leave religious life. So often, nothing is solved by such an action. This reminds me of a very caustic remark of St. Bernard to a woman who wrote to him and suggested that the solution to her problems in religious life was to leave it. The saint wrote to her, "You are either one of the wise or foolish virgins. If you are one of the foolish virgins, you need the community. If you are one of the wise virgins, the community needs you."

The other unfavorable reaction is to remain physically in the community but to cultivate a very passive attitude. This is to say, equivalently, that the best way to avoid being misunderstood is not to do one's own thinking, and never to act on one's own decision. Put into words, this attitude says, "I will simply do only what I am told." This results not only in a joyless existence but even a depressing one.

All his visible life, Christ had to put up with misunderstanding, but never did he allow himself to be discouraged. For example, he was so clear in what he taught and yet even his Apostles did not always understand. Just before his Passion two of the Apostles asked, "Grant to us that we may sit, one at thy right hand and the other at thy left, in thy glory." And when he was about to ascend into Heaven, he was asked, "Lord, wilt thou at this time restore the kingdom of Isreal?" Christ had every human reason to be discouraged with the lack of understanding on the part of the twelve. Yet he did not reject them.

From the way religious act at times, you would think they had never heard that Christ was misunderstood. When you are given a little of the cup of misunderstanding to drink, you turn away as though it were poison. Yet Christ challenges you, "Can you drink of the cup of which I drink?"

Fr. Evoy: It helps to recall that our Lord understands so many of our problems from his own personal experience. In fact, we have few trials, problems, difficulties, or sufferings which Christ does not know from having endured such himself. Indeed, Christ experienced even the most costly consequences of submitting to legitimate authority. Take, for example, what happened when Caiphas recognized that the trial was going badly. He stood up, halted the proceedings, and adjured our Lord to answer his question. "Are you the Christ, the Son of the living God?" In these words, Caiphas, the high priest over all the Jews at Jerusalem, was asking Christ a self-incriminating question. Christ could not answer it directly without passing sentence on himself. Nevertheless, he answered immediately, fully aware that in so doing he was condemning himself to death. One in authority had commanded him to answer a legitimate question, so he was left no alternative, even though to answer it would cost him his life.

Sisters, at times the recollection that Christ had such an experience might prove comforting and reassuring to you, should you be commanded to reveal that which would be self-incriminating.

Christ is next turned over to the civil authority in Jerusalem. Pilate, as he appears in the New Testament, does not present the picture of a really bad man. He stands forth not as a villainous character, but rather as a weak one. Pilate was a man given to compromising his own principles. He was political in the bad sense of that term. Even his final hand-washing gesture was one of cowardly compromise.

In that part of the Empire of Rome only the Roman governor himself possessed the right over life and death. Look at the compromise of Pilate. He said, "I find no cause in this just man" and never retracted that statement. He publicly went on record that Christ was not guilty of the charges made against him. Since Pilate never withdrew from his position that Christ was innocent, where then was his compromise? It was in not being true to his own convictions. Since he said openly that Christ was innocent, his obligation was to free him. Instead, he sought a compromising way out of this obligation.

First, Pilate tried to shirk his responsibility by passing Christ on to Herod. When that did not work out, he tried to release him under the annual Passover custom of freeing some criminal. But the people blocked this compromise by choosing Barabbas instead. Then Pilate had Christ scourged in the hope that this act of cruelty would appease the mob. This failed also. Finally, when the mob's leaders raised the issue of Pilate's loyalty to his leader-in-chief, Caesar, then the Roman governor pitifully played out the rest of the compromising role by melodramatically washing his hands of the whole affair, thus publicly symbolizing that he bore no responsibility for the death of Christ. Under this craven retreat from personal responsibility, Pilate authorized the Jewish leaders to carry out the death sentence.

The escapist pattern here is readily recognized. It is as old as the human race. Simply stated it says, "I will not object, if you will take the responsibility for the consequences." There is food for thought here. A religious, as a human being, is not wholly immune to this danger of shirking the responsibility even for her own behavior. It is well to realize that the temptation to run out on personal responsibility is peculiarly liable to occur in religious life. Frankly, where else could one hide from personal responsibility and have it appear, not as cowardice, but as perfect religious observance? A close study of the man, Pilate, highlights the truth that, to many persons, avoiding the responsibility of having to answer for oneself can be a real temptation.

Fr. Christoph: Pilate, as Father Evoy said, was not really a bad man. He was a weak man. He was reluctant to see Christ, who appeared blameless, put to death. The series of compromises shows this. But each successive yielding brought him closer to what the mob's leaders wanted.

This too often happens with our concessions. We, as religious, sometimes compromise even our principles in the hope of solving a problem, but by doing this we never really achieve what we had hoped to. Moreover, we are less good for having compromised. We are ashamed of ourselves and, at best, we have merely delayed the day of reckoning.

Pilate did not know that there were diabolical forces afoot and that nothing would satisfy the leaders of the people except what Caiphas, the high priest for the year, had prophesied, "It is necessary that one man should die that the people be saved." So Pilate presents Christ, with his thorn-crowned head, his body a mass of bruises from the lashings of the soldiers, hoping to move the mob to pity. But there was no pity. Finally, Pilate says, "You take him now. I am innocent of the blood of this just man." He tried to exculpate himself and put the burden of guilt on the Jews, but it was still his responsibility. There are so many areas where you can convince yourselves that responsibility is not yours. In the last analysis you will have to answer to God for everything that you do, even for what you do under obedience.

I would like to point out a tremendous contrast between Christ's action and that of Pilate's. Father Evoy remarked that Christ signed his death warrant when he acknowledged that he was the Messias, the Son of God. This was the simple truth, and he spoke it. In contrast, when Pilate is called upon to follow his conscience, he manifests himself as a timeserving compromiser. For Christ, death by crucifixion was a most unpleasant prospect. He had to make a choice of conscience, and he made it regardless of the consequences. Saving his life could never be that important to Christ.

In the case of Pilate it was not his life that he was worried about, but his governorship. It was politically expedient that he get out of this scrape without incurring the enmity of either the Jews or his Roman overlords. It is significant that despite his stratagems, in the end he was not successful. History tells us that most probably the decision he made relative to Christ ruined his career. This is just another proof that the weakness of indecision or the readiness to compromise on principle sooner or later proves very costly.

We live in a world of compromise. On all sides we see people yielding on their principles. Even in religious life, some tend to make concessions destructive of their integrity in order to curry favor or to feather their nest. You should not be surprised, sisters, if in dealing with certain religious you find timeserving, double-dealing, and political manipulating. These characteristics may be found in the hierarchy from the highest down to the lowliest official. You ought not be disillusioned by their presence. This is merely the manifestation of one of the more unlovely sides of human nature. But, thank God, most religious do have the courage of their convictions.

Fr. Evoy: Returning to Pilate, we find him a complex, baffling kind of person. He combined intelligence, resourcefulness, and recognition of sham with an ambition that led him to the using of an innocent man to further himself.

Fr. Christoph: Father Evoy implied that we never have any right to use a man. Yet, Pilate used Christ to cement his relationship with Herod. Indeed, they were friends from that day forward. The Roman governor used Christ as a pawn in his effort to keep the Jewish leaders on his side. He used Christ to protect his political security by allowing the Jews to put Christ to death. This is the ultimate in using a person. While few would go to the extreme Pilate did, there are, nevertheless, so many ways in which others can be used to promote one's own ambitions and needs. This kind of behavior should be beneath our contempt.

Fr. Evoy: I should like to add a further note on Pilate. He was a dilettante—one who tends to toy with important things. His characteristic approach seems to be that of "once over lightly" rather than anything like a sustained, serious approach. Almost immediately after Pilate asked Christ, "Are you a king?" he moved away. When he heard Christ speak of truth, he asked "What is truth?" and once more did not remain long enough to hear Christ's answer. Pilate undoubtedly told himself that he was genuinely interested in these most important questions.

Does not an examination of conscience testify that we have, on occasion, acted in somewhat similar manner? We have been led to believe we inquired and really listened to what another person had to say. Yet how seldom, even in religious life, do we really listen to one another.

What did the people present see as they looked at this man who refused to compromise his integrity even to save his life? One person saw a treacherous, dangerous man. Another saw a religious fanatic. Still another saw a man who was completely untrustworthy. It is unlikely that many of them saw the magnificent Christ, because few, if any, were looking for his magnificence.

Does not experience teach that one can see in another largely what one is looking for rather than what is really there. If you look at your sister as one not to be trusted, I think you will find grounds for not trusting her. If you look for defects in Father Christoph and myself, I think you will find some that even we have not seen. You can find a lot of things wrong in another if you look for them. What happens when you look for all that is actually there?

Fr. Christoph: Let us spell out more specifically what Father Evoy has said about what we see in another. Take, for example, the personal interest one may have in another. So often, we say deprecatingly, "What does she see in her?" "What does she see in him?" This says something about our point of view. If we were looking from the vantage point of the other person, we might, too, see the same delightful, wonderful characteristics.

Unfortunately, sisters, at times we look at others in terms of our own needs. For example, if we need a scapegoat, we find one. If we look for the good in another, we almost always can find it. When we have antipathy towards others, often enough it exists because we concentrate on what we dislike in them. This is one way we justify our unkindly attitude. We ought not be looking for the unloving in others. We ought, rather, to be alerted to those things that will attract us to them. With the help of God's grace, and sincerity on our part, we, too, will be able to discover the loveableness which god himself sees in these others.

20 Christ on the Cross

Fr. Christoph: St. Paul says in his letter to the Philippians that Christ "was obedient even to the death of the cross." The life of Christ is the story of his obedience to his Father's will. "It is written at the head of the book that I should come to do thy will, O Lord, my God." So, the Incarnation. At twelve, he said "I must be about my Father's business." Again and again in his public life he says, "I always do the will of him who sent me," and in the Agony in the Garden, "not my will but thine be done." Here is the complete submission of Christ, the God-man, to the will of his heavenly Father. In your vow of obedience your most perfect example is not our Lady who said, "Be it done unto me according to thy will," nor St. Paul who wrote, "Be ye imitators of me as I am of Christ." Rather, it is Jesus Christ himself. In the beautiful prayer which he composed and which is a part of our daily Mass our Lord says, "Thy will be done on earth as it is in heaven." And this, Christ constantly did. When a religious vows to serve God and thus restrict her freedom, she is becoming as Christlike as she can, because if there is any hallmark that distinguishes Christ's behavior, it is his irrevocable commitment to fulfill the will of his Father. And the religious distinguishes herself by a similar commitment.

Fr. Evoy: As Father Christoph just mentioned, when the religious vows to serve God, she is becoming as Christlike as she can at the moment she pronounces her vows. Later on, she will be able to become Christlike also in ways of which she is not then aware. When our Lord frequently repeated that he was doing his Father's will, he was also teaching that doing God's will is not just doing something which is accomplished by a person once and for all. Rather, it is done each day by the carrying out of obediences and opportunities not previously present. No religious can foresee all the implications embodied in her life under vows. A renewal of her vows, then, ought not to be merely a repetition of what she offered on her Vow Day. Her renewal should reach out, as well, to embrace those additional aspects of her commitment which she has since discovered in the day-to-day living of her religious life. Almost every day she will see previously undisclosed opportunities for doing her Father's will.

Fr. Christoph: What Christ said on the cross at the close of his life, "it is consummated," meaning that he had completed the work that had been given him to do, hopefully each religious at the end of every day would be able to say.

As we have already indicated, there is a great amount of concern today regarding religious obedience. When we consider obedience further, we have to be careful that we bear in mind the nature of the virtue as well as the vow. The vow, as you know, is fulfilled when you do what you are told to do within the framework of your rule and constitution. The virtue, going beyond that, prompts one even to anticipate the superior's will and to do all that is commanded generously and fully. Hence the virtue comprehends the vow and goes beyond. This is the perfection of the obedience found in religious life.

We have the example of perfect obedience to the will of God especially in the Passion of our Lord and Saviour, Jesus Christ. Christ did not complain about what was expected of him. He did not carry on a dialogue with his heavenly Father in the Garden. Today, as you are aware, there are those who maintain that the obligation to obey legitimate superiors does not bind unless the subject sees the reasonableness of the command. We discern in this a far cry from the obedience of which Christ has given us the example. As a matter of fact, it is a far cry from any ideal of obedience. For when one says that she will not obey unless she sees the reasonableness of that which is commanded, she is making her own subjective understanding of the command the basis for her obedience. You never do violence to your moral integrity in obeying a superior even when she is unreasonable, as long as she is commanding in an area in which she has authority, and as long as she does not command what is sinful. I do not think that this is always understood because I, myself, see religious unwilling to obey what is contrary to their own judgment. The presumption must be accepted that often the superior has more facts than anyone else upon which to make her decision. Hence the superior's determination should always receive the benefit of any doubt in the mind of the subject regarding the reasonableness of what she has been commanded to do.

It is noteworthy that Christ did his Father's will, manifested through his parents who were inferior to him or through any official in a position to command him even though that power would be used to destroy Christ. We have not the slightest evidence that Christ was not obedient to the law. "Who of you will convict me of sin?" he could ask his enemies, and the people in their turn would say, "Behold he has done all things well." The Passion gets its value, indeed, from the fact that Christ submitted to it in obedience to his Father's will. Blood was made the price of sin and it was up to Christ to offer his blood when and under the circumstances his Father desired. Christ did not like the prospect of the Passion, because in his human nature he is not different from you or me. The natural repugnance he felt towards so horrible a death must have remained with him until his last conscious breath. But he understood this to be his Father's will and he did not hesitate to carry it out.

Fr. Evoy: Implicit in what Fr. Christoph has been saying is that a religious should not obey a command which violates her conscience. Such a command would be something she could not reconcile with her conscience because she would judge it to be actually sinful. But how many directives of legitimate authority are of this nature? This by no means precludes her receiving unwise directives from authority. She might be unable to agree that what her superior maintains is correct. To her any given directive may appear unwise. But the carrying out of something which a religious subject considers unwise need not violate her person. It would be different if, by extreme example, a superior ordered her to step out of the third floor window. But where is the personal violation in obeying what she simply judges to be less wise? Were she convinced that an order would make inevitable the violation of her conscience or that of another, it would be a different matter.

Clearly, the superior's right to exercise her authority is not based on the assumption that what she tells a subject is objectively correct. There is no personal infallibility granted to her by the "grace of office" nor on any other score. In a word, obedience does not presuppose that a superior has to be right, even though she is in conscience bound to try to be right. This means that she has an obligation in conscience to use every reasonable means to be correct. Implicit in this obligation is her duty to really listen to what her religious subjects have to say.

This, of course, bespeaks a real obligation on the part of the subject to tell her superior what in her judgment is needed for wise government, unless she knows from experience that the superior will not listen. In this connection, a religious subject should put to flight once and for all the fallacy that she would be doing her own will rather than God's were she to reveal her abilities and preferences to her superior. After she has told her superior how she feels about an obedience and how she sees it, then she obeys. It should never be forgotten that every religious superior is going to have to render an account to God of how she has employed the God-given talent of her religious subjects. And every religious subject is going to have to render an account to God for giving her superior the requisite information for wise government.

My religious superior might assign me to do something with which I would not agree. I explain this to him. If, after having listened to me, he nevertheless wishes me to do as he indicated, I then carry out his directive. I am not violating my conscience in so doing. Moreover, I so much want my superior to be right, that I try to give him the benefit of any doubt. And there is nearly always some doubt in such matters. Normally, in the area of prudential judgment, things are not black and white.

Fr. Christoph: For example, Father Evoy knows from his own experience that what a superior asked him to do is not going to work. He tells this to his superior. Yet, if the superior wants it done that way, Father Evoy does no violence to his conscience. Normally, no moral principle is involved. What is usually involved is the successful accomplishment of a particular work. But that success is ultimately the superior's responsibility. He will have to answer to God for his persistence in choosing this course of action. Meanwhile, Father Evoy still does no violence to his conscience when he says, "This seems to me unwise, but since this is what you want me to do, I will do it."

Fr. Evoy: The point that needs to be stressed, it seems to me, is that one does not violate his conscience simply by carrying out under obedience something with which he does not agree. For instance, my superior tells me for the foreseeable future every Jesuit member of the university faculty will be in charge of everything. From now on, no one person will any longer be in sole charge of any one thing. I can't believe it. I tell myself that my superior must be joking. I wait for the punch line that never comes. I stop and reflect, then, that this means everyone will be in charge of debating, dramatics, the year book, the paper, and even down to supplying coffee in the faculty lounge. It is most clear to me that this is very unwise. I tell my superior that this is how I feel. He listens, but nevertheless instructs me to go along with this. Does the fact that I still cannot agree mean that I cannot in conscience do it?

Recently, I heard of a superior who went to the sister who was doing the baking for the community and instructed her to make a dozen biscuits out of plaster of Paris. The sister-baker was stunned; "Well, I never," she started to say, and then explained patiently to the superior that one simply did not make biscuits out of such ingredients. "Nevertheless," the superior replied, "I wish you to make them out of plaster of Paris." Sister answered, "Very well if that's what you want," and she proceeded to do as bidden. She could not agree that this was the right way to make biscuits, but she did not violate her own person by agreeing to carry out the direction. Later the superior said, "Thank you, sister. They had to be made out of plaster of Paris since they are for a permanent showcase exhibit of bakery products." We do not have to defend the wisdom of the superior's failure to tell the sister beforehand what the biscuits were to be used for, but the example does point out a kind of situation which can call for obeying against one's better judgment without violation of conscience.

Fr. Christoph: Take an example where the moral issue is clear. A superior involved in an auto accident tells a subject, "I am really in a jam. It is going to look bad for the community. I want you to tell the insurance adjuster that you witnessed the accident and I want you to give him this account. I realize that this is not the truth but we have to protect the community."

Fr. Evoy: The subject here would have no choice. She would have to say, "I am sorry but I cannot in conscience obey you. Even though you are the superior, you have asked me to violate my conscience and I have no choice because the matter is black and white." As we have already told you, regardless of the situation, one may not lie.

Fr. Christoph: Canon Law is very clear that religious are bound, by reason of their calling, to pursue their perfection. Hence it is not a matter of keeping the Commandments but of following the counsels. And this means, in the matter of obedience, that they are to submit themselves to the will of legitimate superiors whenever they are commanded to do that which is not sinful. Hence to refuse obedience, on the basis that the rules and constitution do not bind under pain of sin, is to miss the whole purpose of religious life.

Sisters, you vow to be obedient to all legitimate superiors and not only to the *competent*, legitimate superiors. Your personal success as a religious will be measured according to the degree in which you are faithful in the matter of obedience, not to the degree that the things you do succeed or achieve acclaim. The testimony of Scripture, "The obedient man speaks victory," should encourage you in your life of obedience.

The triumph of Christ is the triumph of obedience. Nothing appeared objectively more disastrous for the kingdom of Christ than his death on Calvary. Yet Christ said to his Apostles, "If I be raised up on the cross, I will draw all things to me." "Because he was obedient," St. Paul says, "God has exalted him and given him a name that is above all names. And at the name of Jesus every knee should bend under the earth, on the earth and above the earth." The obedient Christ is the triumphant Christ. Do you need a greater example to encourage you in your faithful observance of your vow of obedience?

Fr. Evoy: As our Saviour hung dying on the cross, he cried out, "My God, my God, why hast thou forsaken me?" Christ was not here uttering a cry of despair. He was not even complaining. Rather he was praying the twenty-first Psalm which foretold his painful death under obedience. Christ to the last heroically carried out his Father's will.

Fr. Christoph: The crucifix is one of the greatest symbols of Christian asceticism ever presented to mankind. There are so many lessons you can learn from the divine master hanging there. Make them matter for your own meditation.

I should like to close with a quotation from Moses: "Hear, O my people, what I speak to you. Learn my Commandments and fulfill them in thy heart. Thou shalt meditate on them and thou shalt write them on the entry and the door of thy house." No one of us can contemplate the crucifix without being impressed by the *for-me-ness* of the obedience, the humility, the patience, and the longanimity of Christ. As we look upon the crucifix we should be moved to experience within ourselves the desire to be better religious out of love for God. Perhaps, this might be only the love of gratitude. Even if this were so, it could, however, grow into a deep personal love of Christ who is so loveable in himself.

21 Women at the Tomb

Fr. Evoy: When the enemies of Christ were certain he was dead, they approached Pilate, asking for Roman soldiers to seal and stand guard over the sepulcher. Pilate authorized them to employ the Roman guard that had been set aside for their needs.

As the third day following Christ's death approached, his enemies were congratulating each other and celebrating their victory over him. In their merrymaking, their mutual reassurances grew louder as men are wont to do spontaneously when there is a need to drown out mounting fear. Months earlier, when they had demanded of our Lord a sign that he was speaking the truth, he had given them a sign. He said, speaking of his own body, "destroy this temple and in three days I will rebuild it." At the time he was speaking these words, they pretended to believe that he was talking about the temple in Jerusalem. When they were asking Pilate for the Roman guard, they openly admitted that they had understood only too well that Christ was talking about rising from the dead. They insisted that they needed the guards for the sepulcher because this man who had promised to rise from the dead on the third day must have his sepulcher guarded against any tricks of his disciples which might make it appear that he had risen.

As they awaited that third day, their fear grew because he had also said to them, "Honor me before men, and I shall honor you before my Father in heaven; deny me before men, and I shall deny you before my Father in heaven." What if he should rise? No wonder that they were becoming more fearful by the minute. And then the catastrophe! The guards burst in upon their celebration. Still in a state of shock, these Roman soldiers blurted out that this terrifying, ghostlike figure had come on the scene as they were standing guard, that he had easily rolled back the stone to display an empty sepulcher, and that from sheer fright they themselves had become as dead men.

Then the Scribes and Pharisees panicked. In panic men act impetuously and at times foolishly. Pressing a large sum of money on the guards, these Jewish leaders instructed the soldiers to go out at once and tell the people that while they were sleeping at the tomb, the disciples of Christ came and stole his body. So the guards went out and spread this story. Too late did his enemies see the absurdity of the story. Not only was it unthinkable for Roman soldiers to fall asleep on their official guard duty, but had they been asleep, how could they have known what had happened?

What these Scribes and Pharisees learned the hard way, we gladly recognize—that our Lord does keep his promises. If we live for him and his, he will, as he has promised, take us unto himself.

The next incident that I should like you to consider is that of the group of women, hastening, early on the third day, to bestow lovingly the final honors upon our Lord's body. These generous, considerate women had faithfully administered to him throughout his public life. This was to be the final tribute of their love. Right up to this day women have dedicated themselves unstintingly to the service of Christ, spending themselves most generously for him in the ministrations in which women are accustomed to express their love.

There is much we can learn from observing these women as

they hurried toward the sepulcher. They admitted openly that the huge rock guarding the entrance of the tomb was so heavy that all of them together could not move it. This was a difficulty. Notice that it did not stop them. They simply had not yet worked out a way to do that to which even their combined strength was unequal. But nevertheless they kept on. Nothing was going to stop them from serving Christ. What a magnificent example of determination flowing from the real love of real women.

Then, there is the incident with Mary Magdalen. When Mary actually encountered our Lord at the tomb, she did not, at first, recognize him. It is understandable why she failed to recognize him. To begin with, who knew better than she that he was dead? She had been at the foot of the cross when he expired. Hence she was looking for his body, not for someone walking about.

St. John relates that she did not even bother to look at the man to whom she addressed herself. She had eyes only for Christ. Besides, is it unreasonable to assume that heartbroken as she was, her vision would most likely be obscured by tears? Mary said to the one she assumed to be the gardener, "If you know where he is, tell me and I will take him away." We might wonder how a woman would feel that she had the strength to carry Christ's body. We suspect that it did not even occur to her that she would be unable or that it would be even exceedingly difficult to do what she wanted to do for him whom she loved. True love neither calculates nor measures.

When our Lord addressed her by name, perhaps before she even looked at him, she knew him immediately. Not for a moment did she disbelieve that it was really he. All doubt fled before her love. Some are surprised that our Lord said to her, "Mary, do not touch me, for I have not ascended to my Father." This was not telling her that she may in no way express her love for him now. When Christ bids her, "Go tell my disciples," he is saying to her that her love for him is to be manifested not in physical expressions of affection but in faithfully serving him.

This is by no means telling her not to love him. Rather, he is showing her how to express her love. The Gospel tells us that shortly afterwards, Christ permitted the other women to touch his feet. Why not Magdalen? It is my opinion that since Magdalen had become so inclined to link the sensible signs of affection with the sinful, our Lord was telling her that she should not express her love through these channels.

I should like now to call your attention to one final consideration. This side of the grave, we do not have the privilege of seeing our Lord face to face. When we wish therefore to visualize him, we endeavor to represent him as he is. Our relationship with him is such an intensely personal matter that we would not want to picture him to ourselves as some other person visualizes him, and especially not in any unrealistic fashion.

For example, were we to have a special devotion to the Infant of Prague, we would never for a moment mistakenly imagine that the contemporary Christ is still an infant. There is no problem with such a devotion as long as we recognize that we are not therein communicating with the contemporary Christ. Nor is there any problem of a sister's devotion to Christ suffering on the cross as long as she reminds herself that the present Christ is a glorious, risen, triumphant Christ. At the same time, it is of the utmost importance that we never cease to remind ourselves that in the present time we also encounter Christ suffering in each of his suffering and needy members. So you love the gloriously risen Christ in his own Incarnate Person, and you love him also in the person of each of these members.

22 Appearances in the Upper Room

Fr. Christoph: The risen life of Christ is a foretaste of the risen life that is going to be yours. Now is "the space of life between"— so your years on earth, whether they are twenty, thirty, sixty, or even more, constitute just an infinitesimal fraction of the life that is to be yours forever.

We should like now to spend some time with the Risen Christ and his Apostles. We will be with them in the upper room.

When it was late that same day, the first of the week, though the doors where the disciples gathered had been closed for fear of the Jews, Jesus came and stood in the midst and said to them, "Peace be to you!" And when he had said this, he showed them his hands and his side. The disciples therefore rejoiced at the sight of the Lord. He therefore said to them again, "Peace be to you! As the Father has sent me, I also send you." When he had said this, he breathed upon them, and said to them, "Receive the Holy Spirit; whose sins you shall forgive, they are forgiven them; and whose sins you shall retain, they are retained."

Now Thomas, one of the Twelve, called the Twin, was not with them when Jesus came. The other disciples therefore said to him, "We have seen the Lord." But he said to them, "Unless I see in his hands the print of the nails, and put my finger into the place of the nails, and put my hand into his side, I will not believe."

And after eight days, his disciples were again inside, and Thomas with them. Jesus came, the doors being closed, and stood in their midst, and said, "Peace be to you!" Then he said to Thomas, "Bring here thy finger, and see my hands; and bring here thy hand, and put it into my side; and be not unbelieving, but believing." Thomas answered and said to him, "My Lord and my God!" Jesus said to him, "Because thou hast seen me, thou hast believed. Blessed are they who have not seen, and yet have believed." (John 20:19–29.)

Fr. Evoy: In the Scriptural account of the appearances following his Resurrection, our Lord seems almost constrained to repeat the salutation, "Peace, it is I." The Gospels give us no indication that he had done this before the Resurrection. Now each time he appears, he begins with the greeting, "Peace." Our Lord openly proclaims peace after his Resurrection, because the gap between the Creator and the creature produced by sin had now been bridged. Christ had repaired the broken span between God and man. What man had destroyed, the God-man had rebuilt. It is Christ who restored the bridge by means of which man the displaced person could become man the adopted son of God. No wonder that our Lord seems preoccupied with his repeated reassurance of "Peace, it is I."

In effect, Christ is saying to them, "When I am in your midst and you remain close to me, you need never fear. Every danger that could inflict eternal damage has been successfully met. Nothing again need ever hurt you in an everlasting way." He continues to stress the point that where he is there should be peace. Sisters, this point needs to be emphasized. He is telling us not only that we have no *need* to fear when close to him but also that he wants us never to live in fear when he is with us. The contemporary Christ, gloriously victorious over death and sin, bids us to be at peace. As long as he is present in our lives, neither disturbance nor fear nor turmoil can come to us. We recognize the presence of Christ in us by his *peace*.

Fr. Christoph: In the discourse at the Last Supper, Christ had said, "My peace I leave with you; my peace I give to you. Not as the world gives, do I give to you." But the events that followed were very terrifying to the Apostles and certainly not of a nature to instill a sense of peace. Just before our Lord left the supper room to go into the Garden, he had said, "Have confidence, I have overcome the world." Almost immediately afterwards he went out to meet his death. The events of Thursday night and Friday had been most disturbing to the Apostles. No wonder they began to fear. They needed to be reassured.

He comes to his Apostles in his risen life, dissipating all their fears, conferring on them his peace. This peace is the consequence of Christ's restoring their faith and confidence in him. Christ wants his presence always to bring peace. Moreover, any turbulence arising even from spiritual causes should disappear in the impact of his presence. Christ wants you to have this peace, and to share it with others. "Where two or three are gathered together in my Name, there I am in the midst," said Christ. And if he is in their midst, there should be this peace.

Fr. Evoy: Your whole religious life is the living out of the "Yes" of your faith. You have placed your hand in Christ's and thus joined yourself to him who is the Prince of Peace. As long as you faithfully maintain this relationship with Christ, you live in the presence of the Prince of Peace. What is there then to destroy your peace? Death he has triumphed over; sin he has conquered.

Christ in his resurrected life is, in effect, saying to each of you that you should also understand that this peace which he wants for you is a foretaste of what his Father has prepared eternally for you. You live by faith. Faith is a personal commitment. Your faith itself is the source of your peace because it is the link joining you to him who is the Prince of Peace.

Fr. Christoph: Dante wrote, "In thy will is our peace." What Father Evoy has said gives point to these words. When you submit yourself to the will of God, you are making a tremendous act of faith. "The Lord is my shepherd, whom shall I fear?" You put your hand into the hand of Christ and let him lead you whither he will. Then, you are not worried by whatever may happen. Let the winds sweep over the lands; let the thunder clap and the lightning flash! Yes, let the heavens fall! There is interior peace because you know "God's in his heaven, all is right with the world."

Fr. Evoy: St. Paul said:

Who shall separate us from the love of Christ? Shall tribulation, or distress, or persecution, or hunger, or nakedness, or danger, or the sword? . . . . I am sure that neither death, nor life, nor angels, nor principalities, nor things present, nor things to come . . . . will be able to separate us from the love of God, which is in Christ Jesus, our Lord. (Romans 8: 35–39.)

Fr. Christoph: Recall the words of Job:

I know that my Redeemer liveth, and in the last day I shall rise out of the earth . . . . I shall see my God. Whom I myself shall see, and my eyes shall behold, and not another: this my hope is laid up in my bosom. (Job 19:25–27.)

This is the act of faith of an individual steeped in misery. Job also reminds us that "life on earth is a warfare." And yet despite this, note the quality of peace that is his. "Peace," according to St. Augustine, "is the tranquility of order." When you know that God is in his heaven, when you know that things are right between God and yourself, that things are right between you and your fellows, when you feel that in the use of creatures you are aware of your and their *for-God-ness,* then the tranquility of which St. Augustine spoke should be present and you should experience the peace of Christ.

Fr. Evoy: Further reflection on the scene in the upper room brings us to another point, that of trust. Not only is it clear that faith must be a personal commitment, but also inseparably associated with it is trust. After having experienced death, Christ returned to tell us that he had overcome it. We need never again be afraid of death, and it is his desire that we should be at peace. He who went through death and victoriously returned from it conquered sin and its consequences. You really can trust him to see you safely through life's perils. It is trust that stands guard at the threshold of peace.

You do not live very long before you make the discovery that occasional fear is an inevitable part of human experience. On occasions you become upset and worried. You are afraid. Then it is that you trust Christ. In fact, there is no need for making an act of trust in him when you yourself can see that everything is secure. Really, trusting under these circumstances would not make a great deal of sense. It is precisely because your faith involves what is not seen that trust is inseparably connected with it. One thus readily grasps the close association between faith and love.

Your whole scale of values ultimately is drawn from your faith, and your living according to this faith is motivated by your love. Is it not as easy to see how trust is also intimately united with both faith and love? When you live in keeping with your faith, you trust. This trust then becomes a great expression of your love for God. Faith, trust, and love are thus beautifully woven into the fabric of your life.

There are times when your feelings are not in tune with what you know to be so. This is precisely where your trust comes in. Only one afraid is in need of trust. So no matter how afraid, you trust him who still reassures you with his comforting "Peace, it is I."

Fr. Christoph: This visit of Christ with his Apostles in the upper room was also the occasion when he instituted the sacrament of penance. It is fitting that this sacrament should have been given in an atmosphere of peace. Sisters, if there is anything that you should receive from the sacrament of penance, it is peace. You step into the confessional, perhaps quite upset, discouraged, even depressed, and with the absolution of the priest you arise, in a sense, a new person because you have felt the healing hand of Christ upon your soul. The sacrament of penance is a generous act on the part of God Almighty to make it easier to live in the friendship of Christ.

Fr. Evoy: Everything Father Christoph has just said about the effect of the sacrament of penance you accept theoretically. You also know that you must face the experience of confession realistically. The fact is that a real woman does not emerge from the confessional feeling anything but peace. She knows her sins are forgiven because she has confessed them honestly and received the priest's absolution.

Now let me direct your attention to the scene in the upper chamber. Suddenly our Lord was there in their midst. Not one of them doubted that he was physically present in the room. They knew that he was really there because they actually saw him. But what about us? How could we be sure that their experience was not one of mass hysteria?

How considerate it was of Christ to make sure that we would also be certain. It is reassuring to us that later on he would wring a belated acknowledgment from doubting Thomas. But we are most grateful that, in addition to this, he asked on the present occasion for something to eat. When he ate some of the fish before them and handed back the remains of that partly-eaten fish and returned the partly-eaten honeycomb, he provided the evidence we needed. The possibility of mass hysteria vanishes in the face of being presented with a partly-eaten fish and a partly-consumed honeycomb. Now it is highly questionable whether the Apostles watching and listening to him needed any such proof that he was really there. But we needed it and so Christ provided it. How considerate is Christ!

Fr. Christoph: Father Evoy said that this evidence precludes mass hysteria. It also, I think, served to strengthen the faith of the Apostles. They were still disturbed by the event of the previous week. As a matter of fact, when Christ much later was ascending into heaven, we are told, some went away still unbelieving. The incredulity and the earlier lack of loyalty of the Apostles to Christ should have left them humiliated and shamefaced. And they were. But Christ did not hold their record against them. In his words "Receive you the Holy Spirit" there is no reference to their past infidelity. There is nothing about the fact that there were only his mother, Mary, Salome, Mary Magdalen, and John at the foot of the cross. There is nothing about the fact that they ran away when he could have used their support. No. This is the largeness of Christ manifesting itself and teaching us the lesson of magnanimity.

Sisters, when we have been hurt by others our reaction should be modeled on this example of Christ. Here we have a most beautiful instance of the forgiving love of Christ. It is the love of our Lord which takes people as they are with all their weaknesses. He is careful not to remind them of the past. In fact, from the behavior of Christ you would not know the Apostles had a past for which they should have been embarrassed and ashamed.

Fr. Evoy: At first glance, we might wonder at Father Christoph's remark that the faith of the Apostles was strengthened by this appearance of our Lord. In what way did their faith need strengthening? Were they not actually looking at our Lord physically present among them? They were. But it is difficult for us to appreciate their point of view. When you have just seen a person die, you certainly do not expect that person, a few days later, to walk in and talk and eat with you. It is not easy for us to assume their vantage point.

From our own earliest years, the Resurrection of Christ has been a fact assented to on faith. When St. Paul said, "If Christ be not risen from the dead, then our faith is vain," he was not presenting an argument; rather, he was simply stating a fact. In effect, Paul was saying that if our Lord is not risen, then he is not alive; and if he is really alive, then he is risen. This is all clear to us, but we cannot forget that some of these Apostles had seen him expire on the cross and from a safe distance watched as his body was placed in the sepulcher. Moreover, when our Lord clearly foretold that on the third day he would rise again, the Apostles had not understood.

So his appearance in the upper room, eating and speaking with them, did strengthen their faith that the Son of Man had indeed risen from the dead. An unmistakable lesson here is that Christ provides whatever is necessary to enable one to believe, to trust, and to love him. It is so easy for us to forget this. Should extraordinary means be needed, Christ will, we may be sure, have recourse to them. When we fearfully anticipate great dangers, we wonder how our Lord will protect us from them. We do not know. We know only that whatever is necessary for us, he will provide.

Fr. Christoph: However, sometimes our faith is so weak we take every precaution possible against the eventuality we fear. Indeed, we stand in the way of God's providence. We believe, but we trust only up to a point.

Fr. Evoy: Yet, when you stop to look at it, is not your whole religious life the ultimate in trust? You surrender everything. You say, "Take all, including me." Is this not trust? Your life is a living of that trust, a day at a time. You do not see today what you are going to be called upon to surrender tomorrow. You cannot give it to him now because you have not yet seen it. No matter. Tomorrow, you will surrender whatever is asked. This is your life. Really living your religious life is living your trust, in faith, out of love for God.

Fr. Christoph: Sometimes, and this is understandable, God does seem to try your faith to the limit. But he always accompanies these trials with evidence strong enough to persuade you that he is with you, seconding your efforts. The experience of the Apostles in the presence of the Risen Christ was electrifying. It gave them, in a sense, a new hold on life. He ignores their past weaknesses, their infidelity, and their cowardice. He addresses them as he did of old and gives them a new charge—another proof that he has forgiven them, another proof of his love. "As the Father has sent me, I also send you." When you are discouraged, you may ask yourselves: "Does God really care? Does God know what is going on?" Surely, he does. "Fear not, it is I." His presence brings assurance.

From the behavior of Thomas, we can likewise learn a valuable lesson. In human relationships you take a certain amount on faith. Yet, your natural faith is not always strained to the breaking point. Nor should you expect that God will exact from you anything that would put strain on your faith in him. As a matter of fact, Christ teaches you, in the incident involving Thomas, the value of faith, even blind faith.

Fr. Evoy: Father Christoph's remark that God does not act in a way that actually strains your faith needs to be explained. It does not mean that on occasion your faith may not be taxed. Look at doubting Thomas. He was expected to believe merely on the word of the Apostles. Our Lord tested his faith severely. After Thomas had listened to the other Apostles' glowing account of Christ's presence among them, he said, in effect, "This is too much. If I am to believe, then here are my terms: let him present his torn hands to me so that I can examine them and let him permit me to place my hands into the wound in his side."

Fr. Christoph: During the Last Supper Thomas had said, "Show us the Father." Christ, with no show of impatience, answered, "He who sees me sees the Father." It did not sink in very much, did it? There would be no doubt in Thomas' mind about his resurrection if Christ risen from the dead would show himself to him.

Fr. Evoy: The burden of his answer to the challenge of Thomas was, "So these are your terms, Thomas? Very well. I am willing to meet them. Here are my hands. Touch them. And come and place your hand in my side." Thomas was overwhelmed. Now, too late, he realized that he should never have insisted on his own terms.

Our Lord asks you to believe and trust in him because you love him. You really do believe and trust in him. Because you trust him you do not construct, ahead of time, your personal buffer dams "just in case . . . ." You recognize the old "just in

case . . ." pattern. It is alien to what your religious life ought
to be. You placed your hand once and for all in Christ's hand
and, therefore, ought not greatly be concerned with looking out
for yourself. Frankly, you should not have the time to be constantly concerned about yourselves. You should be too busy taking care of his members. This is your life. Just to say that this
is your life does not cost much. To live it is quite another thing.
Really living it is an accomplishment.

Fr. Christoph: The implication of Father Evoy's remark is that
yours should be a realizing faith that penetrates your whole
being. As religious you give concrete evidence of your faith in
God's existence, in the hereafter, in the value of living a life for
Christ, in the worthwhileness of a total commitment. These external evidences are going to be simply a facade if you do not
fully live your religious life.

If faith flowing from your personal love of God does not ani-
mate your whole life; if it is not your motive for getting up in the
morning and for being present at the whole drama of Redemption, reenacted in the Mass; if it does not penetrate the externals
of the liturgy and reach that which is happening on the altar, and
give meaning to your whole day—then your religious life is a
misleading veneer. Your reception of Holy Communion must be
a proof that you are living a life of faith, that you really believe
that this is Jesus Christ uniting himself to the whole Christian
community and especially to those who are receiving the same
Lord at the same time with you.

When you go to your work, whether it be into the classroom,
the hospital rooms and corridors, or wherever it may be, your
steps should be taking you towards this particular activity for
God. Faith must penetrate your entire being so thoroughly that
what St. Paul says—"The just man lives by faith"—becomes a
reality in you.

Fr. Evoy: Faith is your own commitment to Christ. It is your unique commitment. In living that commitment you say your unqualified "Yes" to God. Your act of faith is your free assent to the creed, embracing all those things you have not seen but have believed. This is the faith you strive to live.

Fr. Christoph: "I am the way, the truth and the life. Who follows me walks not in darkness," said Christ. Is that not an astonishing claim? It can be pretty dark sometimes, but if you have your hand in Christ's, you should not be disturbed, you should not be afraid. Nor should you be like Thomas, who refused to believe unless he had the objective evidence before him. Let me remind you what St. Paul, in his Epistle to the Hebrews, says about the content of faith. "It is the substance of things to be hoped for; the evidence of things that are not seen." But there is always enough evidence to enable you to sustain your life of faith. Then, the Apostle goes on to make an act of supernatural faith in order to engender trust and security in you.

Fr. Evoy: There is a very brief answer to the question, "What is your faith?" Our Lord and Saviour has told you. He loves you and this is what he wants you to believe. And your answer in returning that love is, "Yes, we believe what you tell us, just because you tell us that it is true."

23 *Disciples at Emmaus*

Fr. Christoph: We will spend a little more time with the Risen Christ. The apparitions are fascinating. Certainly the one in which he reproaches Peter so nicely and yet obviously has forgiven him everything is arresting.

Commentators on Scripture are wont to find in the triple question of Christ to Peter an opportunity for Peter to make some type of reparation for his triple denial. The fact of the matter is that Christ did say three times to Peter, "Lovest thou me?" And Peter affirmed that he did. Outside of deicide, the worst sin that anybody can commit is knowingly to refuse to acknowledge the divinity of Christ. Peter had said in effect, "I do not even know the man, much less anything about him." Yet Christ confers upon him the primacy.

We may reflect just momentarily upon the goodness of Christ to us. He chooses to save men through men; he uses us who are very conscious of our own weaknesses and our limitations as the instruments through which he is going to save men. He is so big and so large-hearted that he takes us as we are and he does not throw our past before us. Scripture emphasizes this. We ought not, therefore, to live in the past, nor should we be afraid of the past. What we ought to be concerned about is our attitude towards Christ today. What we should try to envision is our role in the apostolate to which we have committed ourselves. It is a real feeling of relief to know that Christ has this very forgiving love for men because our shortcomings embarrass us at times. Maybe we are a little embarrassed about the generosity of Christ, but there it is, and it is there for us.

Fr. Evoy: I think our ordinary experience verifies what Father Christoph has just been saying about the forgiving nature of love as he viewed it in Christ. We find that when we dislike someone, so many things that person does tend to annoy us. On the other hand, when we really like someone, though that person's defects might momentarily bother us, they somehow do not really detract from that person. Does our Lord frown disapprovingly at us for the sins we have committed and contritely confessed throughout our lives? No. Because we have honestly confessed them and sincerely endeavored to change our lives.

Fr. Christoph: We would not want to minimize the gravity of sin, but for the most part our sins are according to our fallen nature—uncharity, because we are self-centered; gluttony, because we do not put a limit on eating or drinking; lust, because the flesh follows a natural drive; laziness, because we want to seek our ease; and so forth. We are not minimizing the seriousness of sin, but we are emphasizing the fact that Christ knows us with our weakness.

Here we are going to consider the story of Christ's appearance to the two disciples on the road to Emmaus. In order to understand the feelings of these two, we should recall that all the disciples seem to have been disappointed and dejected. They were disappointed in Christ because he did not restore the kingdom of Israel. They must have been let down by the prospects of a very drab existence from here on, after having enjoyed the magnetic personality and fellowship of Christ. The mother of

James and John had asked if her sons might sit at his right
and left hand. Now there did not seem to be any kingdom in
which to sit. Their dream world had collapsed. They had
planned in terms of a theocratic kingdom and it had all come
to nothing. The mood of the Apostles is well expressed by the
disciples on the road to Emmaus when they said, "And we
thought that it was he who would restore the kingdom of Israel."

These two disciples separated themselves from the group. Probably they thought, "There is no point in sitting around here.
Why don't we do something? Let us just get away from all these
memories." And Emmaus came to mind. At least it was a place
to go and something to do.

There is a strong temptation whenever you have the blues to
get away from it all. Do not misunderstand; there are socially,
morally, and spiritually acceptable escapes, and to seek them is
at times legitimate. When I am tired, perhaps I may want to lie
down. This is an escape from some type of fatigue. Maybe, when
I am wearied after teaching, I just want to enjoy some light
conversation. Perhaps my head is in a whirl. I have been reading a technical book on one of the subjects I am teaching or a
deep spiritual book. I need some relaxation. My eyes are not
tired so I read a novel or mystery story. There is nothing unbecoming about this. I am not running away because I am deso-
lated or because I just cannot stand life. I am looking for a little
reasonable variety to relieve my fatigue.

But these two disciples were not merely seeking relaxation;
they were running away. They were leaving Jerusalem which in
Hebrew means the vision of peace. (The temptation to flee Jerusalem, when one is desolate, is a temptation which I believe
has touched most of us at some time or another.) They were
unable to accept a situation which did not correspond to their
expectations. They were unable to face their real world so they
sought escape in flight.

Fr. Evoy: It seems rather strange that as they were walking away from Jerusalem and all the activities concerning Christ, it was Christ they were speaking of. They were even astonished when our Lord asked them what they were talking about, as if to say, "What else would we be talking about?" Then they told him how they had received something of a fright that very morning. Some of the women in their number, they said, had gone to the sepulcher at dawn and returned saying that the tomb was empty and, moreover, the women claimed they had been told by an angel that Christ was risen from the dead.

What is really surprising in these two disciples is that their preoccupation with Christ seems to have been rather impersonal, almost academic. Apparently, they were downcast because of what had happened to their kingdom rather than because of what had happened to Christ. There is no indication whatever that they even had to fight off the urge to go out to Golgotha and examine the sepulcher for themselves. In fact, at this moment they were walking away from Jerusalem. Among other things, sisters, were they not demonstrating that it is quite possible for someone to do a good deal of talking about our Lord, without feeling any deep personal involvement with him?

However, the fact that we cannot approve of their going away does not mean that every tactical retreat is improper. Rather, as Father Christoph indicated, there are occasions when we rightly take time off from our normal activities to read a light book, watch T.V., listen to a radio, or just sit. But the all-important point is that we do not leave Christ in order to relax. We take him with us. Is there any good reason why we should really leave our Lord when we feel the need for some good relaxation?

Fr. Christoph: Your need is a change of fantasms, not a running away from reality. This is not abandoning your responsibilities. You are still quite aware that after a time you will return to them. The two disciples did not seem to be of this mind. They were, as Father Evoy said, running away from Christ, and all the related memories, and presumably were seeking some way out of their real situation which brought them despondency and discouragement.

Fr. Evoy: Something else suggests itself here in this Gospel account. We can largely thank Protestant theologians for having given considerable attention to Christ's promise "Where two or three are gathered together in my name, there am I in the midst of them." In these words our Lord was talking about a presence by which he would really be with them and yet which was neither the Eucharistic presence nor God's sustaining and cooperating presence in all created things. Actually, it is not clear what the precise nature of this other presence is. The important point is that he actually is present in such a situation. Was he, in fact, making use of the journey to Emmaus in order to demonstrate visibly such a presence? Even though these two disciples were walking away, they were occupying themselves, no matter how impersonally, with thoughts of Christ and were speaking to each other about him. And as they were doing so, Christ joined them, although they did not then recognize who he was.

Fr. Christoph: The commiseration of Christ is evidenced here. He loves and feels for us. If the disciples had been talking about the latest type of entertainment at Emmaus and had not been concerned about the events that had so recently occurred at Jerusalem, we would see no reason why Christ should have appeared to them. But because they were really concerned and talking about him, Christ kept his promise. He was there in their midst. They told him the story of what had transpired in Jerusalem as though he were unaware of these events. And in their remarks their weakness of faith betrayed itself. They said, "But we were hoping that it was he who should redeem Israel, and this is the third day already since these things have come to pass." There was no indication that they believed what they heard, much less that they accepted his divinity. So he spoke to them to strengthen their faith.

Christ speaks specifically of their failure to understand what the prophets had foretold of him. Here he is also calling our attention to the fact that if we understood Scripture better, we would have a fuller understanding of salvation history. There is no question but that a deeper knowledge and understanding of the Old Testament as well as the New Testament will give us a much better appreciation of Christ. God comes in the Word made flesh, but he also comes in the *word* of Scripture. This is an aspect of spiritual reality being emphasized today. Christ's reproof "Oh, foolish ones and slow of heart to believe all that the prophets have spoken" is too often deserved today.

Fr. Evoy: Only later did these two disciples recognize the comforting experience which earlier had been theirs. Afterwards they could say, "Were not our hearts burning within us, when he was explaining to us the Scriptures?" Later they recalled the warmth which had been theirs while he spoke. When we hear or read Scripture, we ought to do so *listening*. It should be a listening to God talking directly to us through his word. And it may be that when we do truly *listen* to Scripture in this way, only later will we be aware of the warmth that was ours when we were attending to his word.

When Christ began speaking to the two Emmaus-bound disciples, he chided them for not having understood the Scriptures. Had they actually read the Scriptures? Certainly. Christ would not have rebuked them for not having understood what they had not even read. What our Lord finds fault with is that they had not understood the Scriptures. I wonder if his reprimand to these two was not on the score that they failed to understand, precisely because they did not view the Scriptures as God's personal revelation to them.

Fr. Christoph: I should like to develop further the mental attitude of the disciples, which we have already mentioned. Do you know from what they were suffering? Disillusionment. In the analysis of the discernment of spirits, St. Ignatius reminds us not to make vital decisions when we are really depressed. Not to change our course of action, nor our behavior, nor do anything we may regret afterwards. When we are depressed, we tend to take a defeatist attitude toward everything. What is worse, we may act upon this feeling. Sisters, I think that disillusionment is just part of growing up. To be able to accept it without being so crushed that you cannot rise again is an indication of maturity.

We see things in the Church that should not be. For example, we may at times see pettiness on the part of ecclesiastics; at times, mediocrity on the part of religious. Superiors who seem to play favorites appear dishonest in their behavior. A few will not even refrain from stooping to what looks like lying and cheating. And we may see companions who appear to have the same shortcomings.

And when we look at ourselves, the aspirations, the zeal, the love that we had as youth seem all too often to have disappeared. Instead, in us there is an indifference, a coldness, a callousness, even a selfishness—a kind of contentment with just getting by. When we compare these two pictures, the before and the now, we are disappointed that we have not measured up to our own expectations. This is to suffer disillusion.

Most of us can take mild types of disillusionment. But we are only too well aware of what looks like vindictiveness, smallness, cruelty, pride, and the desire to dominate in some religious women. And when these traits manifest themselves it is sometimes more than human nature can accept. These same religious have been at Mass and Communion and have received the same Lord; they are members of the same Mystical Body, and yet at times they are not on speaking terms with one another! Or an hour after they have been in the embrace of the divine friend,

they are ready to do battle with a fellow religious. It is so hard
to understand. The intense suffering in others caused by these
traits is more than should be tolerated. Closing our eyes to the
presence of such hurtful individuals within religious communities is not the pattern dictated by our love for our community.
Rather, we frankly face whatever is hurtful in the community
or in the Church and do what we can to eliminate such damaging elements from both. We do not love the community or the
Church less because of such corrosive factors.

Fr. Evoy: It is perhaps the very witnessing of these sins that
brings into strong focus your love for your religious life. Because
you care, it is painful for you to have to recognize that a religious
you love is notably less than her best self. Also, because you care
about your community, you find it painful to acknowledge failings which keep it from being what it should be. You love your
community far too much for that. There is no question here of
your sitting in judgment on the personal sins of your fellow religious. You are not tempted to play God in this fashion. But the
pain you experience because as a result of such failings your
community is not operating at its best is the evidence that you
do love it. You ought to do everything in your power to love
your sisters with a genuine love and work in every way possible
for their betterment and that of your community. Accordingly,
you care too much simply to turn and walk away toward
Emmaus.

Fr. Christoph: In my caring about the community I have to reflect upon my own attitude toward the rules and constitutions,
the discipline of the house, and especially my spirit of charity. I
have to answer to God for my own conduct and for the conduct
of others to the extent that my example has been hurtful to them.
I think that nothing could be more damaging to me in the
presence of Almighty God than to have to admit that I lessened

the zeal of a fellow religious, that I scoffed at her devotion, that by my own conduct, by word and example, and particularly by my detraction and calumny I really hurt her.

I am not a social isolate in the community. Of necessity my conduct must have an impact upon those around me. If I have followed the advice or the example of those less good, God is going to take me to task for doing so. I must answer for any scandal taken. But the scandal giver will also have to answer to Almighty God, and if I give scandal I must answer to God, especially if I have been the source of disillusionment to any of my religious companions.

I said that I am not a social isolate; neither are you. You have an impact on those about you; you have an obligation to be a source of inspiration and edification to them. You have to bring Christ, and Christ alone, to your companions. If you bring anything less, you are certainly responsible for any degree of the disillusionment your fellow religious may experience.

I think that the defection of some religious has been the result of disillusionment. I have been told by ex-religious that the spirit of the community, the way the community lived its life for Christ, the observance of the constitutions and rules, and especially the interpersonal behavior of members of the community were much less than they expected and so they left. This would not necessarily justify leaving. But to the extent that their allegations were true, those responsible will have to answer to God.

Fr. Evoy: I recall a remark once made to me by a religious. "Whenever someone who has lived in the same house with me leaves the community I examine my conscience." I think he was referring to the fact known to all of us, that some religious have not only been disillusioned about the actual life in religious communities but, moreover, have been repeatedly hurt by their fellow religious. By no means are coldness and uncharitableness confined completely to those outside religious life. In fact, it seems accurate to say that among those who leave religious life are numbered persons who have been treated so unfairly that in a sense they were pressured to leave. The responsibility for their defection would seem to be not wholly theirs.

There are some religious who are very lonely. Does not their very existence point an accusing finger in our direction? Sisters have left a community after finding the life there one of great loneliness. When each of these persons entered, she gave up the family she might have had if she had married. When she joined the community, she was told that she was becoming a member of a religious family. If others had really tried to love her, to like her, to be close to her, and to be real to her, they would have lessened her loneliness. If her loneliness was not notably decreased, ought not her companions examine their consciences?

Fr. Christoph: There has been considerable discussion recently about individuals leaving religious life because of a feeling of nonacceptance. It has been remarked of some of these that they were street angels and house devils. Perhaps they became street angels because they were accepted by externs. Perhaps bad example and ill treatment helped make them house devils. I am not saying that other factors are not involved. I merely wish to emphasize what Father Evoy has said. Each of these women gave up the warm personal interrelationships she might have had; and if they did not find warm acceptance in religious life, they may have been socially starved. In their hunger for companionship, they turned to externs.

Fr. Evoy: We have to be realistic when we talk of a warm acceptance of others in a community. This warm genuine acceptance is really love, and the love we are speaking of is not some detached filmy cobweblike substance floating about in the air. It is real and can be intensely personal.

When you talk most realistically about loving your sisters in the community, you are speaking about yourselves as you are and about them as they are. For instance, you may find it a most uncomfortable task to approach and speak to a sister you do not know well. She may be bitter and show it. Nevertheless, you determine to get to know her. Out in the yard, from a distance, you take one look at her face and you get that sinking feeling in your stomach. You cannot do it. Not today. Maybe tomorrow. But meanwhile you feel you will have to love her pretty much as an unknown and from a considerable distance.

In reality it is very difficult for many of you to love certain of your sisters. One reason why it is so difficult is that some of them have become ensnared in a vicious circle. Because a certain sister appears never really to have had the warming experience of being loved, she really does not know what *love* is. So if in the past she ever tried to love others, she has long since ceased such efforts. Out of fear she has closed herself off from all intimate personal contact with others. She feels that she simply cannot permit anyone to get personally close to her. As you look at her, you might sense this. You even suspect that were you to move in close to her, thus leaving yourself highly vulnerable, she might from fear turn on you. The recognition that she could be motivated to do so out of fear, rather than viciousness, would not prevent her behavior from being exceedingly hurtful.

Thus when you realistically view this business of loving such a person, it is a perilous undertaking. Moreover, you are sure you could never find a certain sister so personally attractive that you would want her for your special friend. To ambition that would be unrealistic. But you can try to understand her, to be courteous and even gracious to her, to forgive her and even to like her. You need not approve of everything a sister does in order to be able to like her, any more than you have to subscribe to everything your close friends do.

This matter of loving someone in the community who seems not very lovable to you is in need of further elucidation.

Occasionally a sister seems cantankerous, as though just lying in wait for someone to express an opinion before pouncing on that person. There are sisters who seem bent on getting into an argument. You might find yourself retreating from such a situation on the score that there seems to be no point in letting something unpleasant get started. You are not obliged to play a role of make believe. You do not have to hold a masklike smile on your face.

Nor ought you, in any way, be untrue to yourself in order to win someone over in the beginning of friendship. You might even have to let a person know that you are never to be used. Neither need you express your affection through the ways urged by the other person. You must judge whether the expressions would lessen in any manner the personal integrity of either one of you. You seek to find wholly acceptable expressions of your love for her. And you can begin to come close to liking her by correctly and charitably interpreting her behavior.

Instead of viewing her as certainly vicious, mean, or spiteful, you at least try to see her as frightened, uncertain, and trying safely to withdraw. You endeavor to interpret her behavior as not saying to you, "What presumption! What forwardness! What effrontery you have," but rather as, "No involvements for me. Please go away." But you would be less than realistic if for a moment you thought that trying to give her behavior the best possible interpretation would remove the hurt she can give you.

There is just no way to be open to others and remove all possibility of being hurt. In a word, it takes courage—great courage even, to start to love some people. Yet if you can ever get through with your love to such a person so that she accepts your love, that love will begin to melt the bars of her personal prison so that she can come forth and begin to live rather than go on just existing.

Fr. Christoph: And you should be aware of the possibility that if she is hurt badly enough, there is no guarantee that she ever will come out.

Fr. Evoy: Returning to the need to examine your conscience concerning her condition, you hope that you will never have to tell yourself, "She remained in self-imprisonment because of me." If you have really tried to love her, that knowledge will be a source of consolation to you regardless of what happens to her. She is your sister whom God wants you to love.

Fr. Christoph: St. Luke tells us that as they neared the village the two disciples said, "Stay with us, for it is getting towards evening and the day is far spent." There was something about this man that made them reluctant to let him go on. His very presence comforted and encouraged them. Such is the true impact of Christ on those close to him.

Fr. Evoy: The reason they said, "Stay with us," was that Christ gave every indication that he was intending to go on. Why would he give them the opportunity to press him to stay with them? For one reason, because Christ is a perfect gentleman, and a gentleman never imposes on people. In his dealings with you, Christ does not force an entrance. He will wait patiently until you invite him to join you. He wants to be wanted.

24 Suscipe: The Contemplation for Love

Fr. Christoph: The whole purpose of man is to praise, to reverence, and to serve God and so merit his friendship. We are lovers. The goal of every man, especially of every religious, should be to live a life of love that in its most perfect form consists in a complete surrender to the Beloved. The more a religious loves, the more she gives herself. Father Evoy has mentioned several times that in the vows you give yourselves unconditionally to Almighty God.

St. Ignatius, reflecting upon the love-motivated pursuit of man's goal, composed the beautiful little prayer that is familiar to all of you. "Take and receive, O Lord, my entire liberty, my memory, my understanding, and my whole will. All that I am and have Thou hast given me and I give it back to Thee to be disposed of according to Thy good pleasure. Give me only Thy love and Thy grace, with these I am rich enough and ask no more."

Fr. Evoy: Notice again the words, "Take and receive . . . my entire liberty." God has made each of you a free being. To be free is your nature; freedom is inseparable from you. At your birth you already possessed your human nature and so you had the power to act freely, but you did not yet have the *use* of that power. For example, when as a child you played "Blindman's Bluff" or some other such game, you had the *power* to see, but as long as the blindfold covered your eyes, you did not have the *use* of that power. The employment of your freedom developed gradually as you matured toward adulthood. As the years passed, you did more of your own thinking and more of your own deciding. You did more determining of your own course of life.

In view of these considerations, the nobility of your religious life becomes manifest. In taking your religious vows you freely turned over to God's disposal the freedom which he built right into your nature. Under this religious dedication of your vows, you contracted for the rest of your earthly life to want what God wants. In this commitment you declared that you would continue courageously as a person in your own right to do your own thinking and your own deciding, but henceforth you were determined to operate within the guidelines of what your superiors, under God, directed you to do within the bounds of their proper authority. In a word, you placed the freedom which was yours as a human person completely at the service of God.

Fr. Christoph: A peculiar thing about this commitment is that it leaves you free to worry about it. If you had to do what you do out of fear or because of some physical compulsion, your actions would not be what Father Evoy has just described as the wonderful thing about vocation—that of a person freely giving self to God out of love.

Fr. Evoy: It is not difficult to detect the danger, disguised as an act of abandoning love, which could lurk here within inadequate people. There could be a temptation for such persons to avoid being responsible for themselves by wanting to return to God not just the *use* of the power of self-determination, but the *power itself* of choice. It would mean for a woman religious that she ceases her own evaluating and her own deciding, and thus as a kind of religiously garbed dehumanized and depersonalized robot, she becomes a nonfree slave for God.

An inadequate sister could become a victim of such an error and regard it as an heroic act. She might have little awareness that she was endeavoring to please the Creator by destroying his highest visible creation—a free human person. To deny the nature God has given her would, of course, be to deny God, even though she did not realize it. When a religious avoids such a pitfall, she dedicates—because she freely chooses to—her voluntary actions to God each day of her life. She lives so as to please him rather than herself. She lives this dedication hourly because she chooses thus to give God, out of true love, the greatest gift possible—herself.

Fr. Christoph: This dedication is to be realized within the framework of the congregation to which you belong and to which you have given yourselves irrevocably. This is never, in any sense, a diminution of yourselves as persons, because you are your best selves when you realize your greatest potential. This is achieved in giving yourself to God freely, placing yourself completely at his disposal. Lack of satisfaction—the absence of the hundredfold in your vocation—more often results from failure to make the gift complete. You have kept something for yourself and that very fact renders your gift to God less self-fulfilling. You fear "Lest, having him, you have naught else beside."

Fr. Evoy: Father Christoph's point that your religious dedication is never a diminution of yourself as a person needs to be emphasized. The peril of erroneously depersonalizing must always be guarded against. Sisters, this calamity has, in fact, happened to religious. It would be unrealistic to fail to regard this as a real danger. You can hide in religious life from your own personal

responsibility and so escape the peril of the perilous thing which
is human freedom. Unfortunately you can mistakenly call it
obedience when you abandon self-accountability by determining
that you will let superiors do *your* thinking and *your* deciding.

What a tragic thing to be able to mislead yourself into thinking that you are serving God by performing a kind of psycho-
logical witchcraft on yourself that reduces your sublime human
person to the level of an animated sponge. You thus would use
the freedom God has given you to change yourself into a living
automaton in order better to serve God! Never! Because you
have been created a free self-determining person, you shall always
be accountable for your life. Because you are fallible, you can
make mistakes. Living is a risky business. May you have the
courage always to accept it fully and to continue to be fully
accountable for living your life.

Fr. Christoph: I might add that this is freedom under law. You
dedicate yourselves and give your freedom to God and you exercise it now within the framework of his law. What is this law? It
is the law of love.

Fr. Evoy: Let's make the preposterous supposition that I were
to come to Father Christoph, my superior, and say to him, "Please
tell me what I should think about this trip and please decide
whether I should ask permission for it or not?" I think I know
what the burden of his answer would be, once he had recovered
from the shock. He would be almost speechless as he tried to
explain to me that he could not take over my responsibility for
being me. For him to do *my* thinking for me or to make my
decisions for me would simply be unthinkable. And if I were to
add, to his still greater shock, "But I am afraid that unless you
tell me these things I will be doing my *own* will rather than
God's will," I think I could anticipate Father's reaction. He
would say, not too calmly, I'm afraid, "Father, don't make a

mockery of obedience. You must always freely decide what you think about it, and then decide whether or not you are justified in asking for it. The important thing is that you want to do what you know, or at least think, would be most pleasing to God."

I think that if Father Christoph judged it necessary, he would further point out to me that two persons—my superior and I— must answer for everything I carry out under obedience. Father Christoph knows well that as a human being I am going to be frequently unsure of what is the right thing to think or to do. Even though he is a superior, he also is often unsure of what is best. Never for a moment, I am certain, would he disregard the dignity which is mine as a self-accountable human being by attempting to do my thinking and deciding for me. Were he by a most unlikely possibility to do so, he would indeed show a lack of respect for the person God has made me. In such a case he would be treating me as if I were either less than human or less than an adult, neither of which is becoming. Yet, I do not think we are crying "havoc" here just for the sake of talking.

This basic trust needs to be stressed because it is so easy, for women especially, to exercise authority over children. For the most part it is not until girls become adolescents that they prove troublesome to women who exercise authority over them. Were they to be kept children, such trouble would be unlikely. And it is religious life which offers the opportunity, under incorrect but sincere notions of obedience, for a superior to unconsciously regard her subjects as children. The pattern is unmistakable. The sisters in her community are given to understand that they are to ask, each and every time, for every small permission. It goes without saying that permission is required for a surprisingly large number of things.

For example, after years in religion, permission may be required even to write a letter. In fact, more than one permission may be needed, as additional permission may be needed for the writing materials. Some of you may be incredulous that such

childlike treatment still exists. Regrettably there are instances
where such permissions are never given as monthly or semi-
annual or much less general permissions, but are required each
and every time a letter is to be written.

We have long realized that it is unfortunate indeed that we
have had to use the terms "mother-daughter" for the superior-
subject relationship. It makes it so easy for a woman superior to
say "my daughter" and really mean "my children." If they are
thought of by her as children, then they must at times be told
what to think and what to choose. We tell a little girl that she
should hold that history is important even though all those
people are dead, and we tell her that she should choose to go to
school even though she can see no point in it. And the only way
one can tell an adult also what to think and what to choose is
by acting as if the adult were a child. The whole picture of regarding religious subjects as dependent children is unrealistic.
It is only *make believe.*

In some instances, superiors without any clear idea of the
tragedy taking place have treated women religious from the
novitiate on as if they were just beginning their religious life and
so, in a sense, were children. But they were not just beginning
their religious life. They had been living a religious life since
their baptism. They were beginning not their religious life but
only their community life. They were young adults or nearly
adults when they were novices. They were not children. But the
tragedy is that because some sisters in charge continued to treat
them like children, they actually began to *feel* like children.
Young adults can be that uncertain of their adulthood.

How many women religious have in this way allowed themselves to be prevented from becoming real women? How often do
we find in religious life, not real women, but really older
girls. Why? Is it not, in part, because, from misguided zeal, they
have been treated as though they were not yet mature women?
Some elder religious and some superiors have not only kept

them perennial children but also, I am afraid, unknowingly helped depersonalize them by blocking the growth of so much that was uniquely theirs. Fortunately, despite such a pattern, some have developed themselves into real women.

Fr. Christoph: There is a real danger here, too, that you not only have depersonalized the individual but you have made religious life impossible. The individual, making one last attempt to preserve some bit of her personality, is in a sense forced to leave the cloister. This restricting pattern is completely out of harmony with our analysis of obedience and the nature of freedom and what should be done with liberty. You gave your life to God, and you are going to operate now as free persons within a framework you value and prize, the one in which God wants you to operate. You do not cease to be free when you do what your superiors tell you to do. You have freely consented to subject yourselves and this is an exercise of freedom. There must always be the free consent of the individual, else there is no human act.

Fr. Evoy: Those of you who have been superiors know well that superiors, particularly younger superiors, are often unsure, often uncertain. This is one reason why superiors need so much supportive help from their community. Typically, a real woman superior does what she thinks and feels is the right thing.

It is precisely because the feeling that she might have to give an account is such an uncomfortable one that the inadequate superior, as a defense, could unwittingly come to regard her subjects as children. One need not answer to a child for what one does. And so, in the name of God's service and smooth government she can destroy that which God has made. If Sister Christoph says to Sister Evoy, "Dear, this is the way you fold these linens and arrange this table," she is saying either that I am mentally retarded or a child. It is difficult for her to feel that I am mentally retarded in view of the education to which I have been exposed. So she must be thinking I am a not yet wholly responsible child. If she keeps this up day after day, the time will come when to the extent that I am inadequate, I will have been conditioned to the point where I, myself, will begin to wonder whether I *am* a child.

This is the insidious aspect of this whole business of keeping subjects children. It can be done by an insecure woman to her religious subjects, and some of these subjects could misguidedly permit it to be done to them, and neither superior nor subject would clearly see the incredible damage resulting from it.

Fr. Christoph: Since God operates through secondary causes, through superiors and the like, you leave yourselves open to the possibility that those in authority may abuse it. We have already spoken at some length on this point. Because you are so vulnerable, you realize how much faith is required to say, "I give you, God, my entire liberty."

Fr. Evoy: This offering is the beautiful expression of your dedicated life. When you say, "Take and receive, O Lord, my entire liberty," you are not at all saying, "From now on I will cease to be free, from now on I will have no liberty." Quite the contrary! What you are really saying is "From now on I will exercise my liberty for you. I shall, with your help, take full responsibility for doing my own thinking and making my own deliberate choices and, within the framework of religious obedience, freely and responsibly live for you." Moreover, you readily acknowledge that in many things you will remain uncertain, because you cannot eliminate the risk of error in your thinking and choices, since such risk is embodied in human freedom.

Fr. Christoph: Father Evoy said that you cannot take the risk out of human freedom. I am sure that the majority of superiors, especially the older ones, may say, "Well, Father, you do not know these people. Some are imprudent; you cannot give them too much rope because they are going to hang themselves. What you say is fine in theory, but in the practical order we have to check them."

It is nonsense to say that it is impractical. Actually, we are not saying that each religious is always free to do just what she thinks is the right thing. We have never said that. Each religious puts forth her best effort while keeping it within the framework of good order. If something is evidently outside of the constitutions or the work of the congregation, and sister says, "Well, I am going to do it anyway," her attitude would not make good sense. There has to be a recognition of order. I do not think that the superior is going to have many subjects, or necessarily any subjects, who are going to make irreparable mistakes in these areas.

They will make the seeming mistake of doing something "my way" rather than the superior's way, and that is about all. There may be a dozen ways to "skin a cat," and the superior's way is one way. "But I choose this particular way of doing it. It may be a little more awkward; it may take a little more time, but it is *my* way," says a subject. Those in the position of authority very frequently do not give the sisters under them credit for being able to make an intelligent judgment. What a waste of potential! If we think for them long enough, a time will come when they will give up thinking for themselves. The potential of the sisters can only be exploited in an atmosphere where initiative, ingenuity, imagination, and creativity are allowed expression. The dynamic nature of society must not be lost sight of in religious life.

Fr. Evoy: Though I dislike the term "brain-wash" I think it is not too strong to characterize what some superiors can do to some religious. On the other hand, if religious are really trusted, is that not dangerous? Can they not make mistakes, even costly mistakes? Yes, they can. Moreover, it is a reasonably safe prediction that where religious are trusted to do their own thinking and to make their own decisions, some of them will make mistakes, perhaps even serious ones. This is the calculated risk always to be found in exercising human freedom.

But cannot the superior also make mistakes, perhaps even costly ones? Did we not say that this is one reason a superior needs the loyalty of her subjects, precisely because at times, being unsure, she can do the wrong thing? She does not *have* to be right. No one has seriously and intelligently maintained that because she is a superior, she cannot make even grave mistakes. She is a human being, exercising her freedom in honestly trying to do the wise thing and the right thing. She can still in good conscience make mistakes.

It is so important for you as religious subjects to recognize that your superior can be wrong, and for her to recognize it also. I think all of you have heard of a thing called the superior's "grace of office" explained as God's guarantee that she will always know, in matters of her office, exactly what God's mind is. Don't laugh. That has been seriously maintained, though on what grounds it would be difficult to imagine. Because a superior is as liable to error and mistake as is a subject, you see also what a great injustice it would be to attempt to place on her shoulders the responsibility which each of you has in terms of self-accountability.

I keep coming back to the thought that at the Last Judgment we might imagine a religious giving her account to our Lord in these words, "Dear Lord, please talk to my superior." To which he answers, "I'll talk to your superior later. Now I want you to give an account for what you have done and failed to do in your religious life."

Fr. Christoph: You insist that your superiors accept you as you are with all of your defects. Father Evoy says this is a two-way street. This means that you accept your superiors with all their defects. Remember, they did not ask to be superiors! Before you complain too much about a superior, you should be sure that you come to court with clean hands, that is, that you do not demand perfection in a superior, while at the same time expecting the superior to take you as you are with all your defects.

Fr. Evoy: Can you acknowledge in your superior the capacity to err? In practice, this means acknowledging that she can honestly be in error in her judgments as superior. This is your admission that she does not *have* to be correct in everything she does as superior. It concedes that you do not demand perfection of her. You would very much like your superior to return the compliment. The fact is that you do not *have* to be right either. You are well aware you can be honestly mistaken in your judgments. Once you are reassured that your superior recognizes your right to run the risk of making a mistake, you can stop holding your breath. The important thing here is that you are able rightly to presume that the superior actually trusts you to follow your conscience, even though you cannot be sure that, in so doing, you will avoid error. This presumption permits you the experience of the freedom to make a mistake. If you were free to act only when you were certain, you would not be free to function properly as a human being.

Fr. Christoph: St. Ignatius said, "Take my memory." Many of the things I remember I surely would like to forget, yet I say, "Take my memory." When I say this, I mean to give to God everything in my past. But I do this with abundant confidence born of faith and experience. Born of faith, because God has said, "If your sins be as numerous as the sands of the sea and as red as scarlet, I will make them white as snow." Born of experience, because of his forgiving love shown to the woman taken in adultery, to the paralytic, to St. Peter, to the good thief on the cross, and to sinner-saints down the ages. I am not afraid to offer God even my sinful past because I trust in his forgiveness. I hope that when I show the cinders of the past, my whole burnt offering—which is not much to offer to Almighty God—he sees the totality of it. He sees that here and now I am offering to him my life, the good and the regretted evil. I am offering my life as it is. I know he is good enough to accept all of it, including those elements of which I am not at all proud.

Fr. Evoy: No real woman finds it hard to surrender her past. As Father Christoph just said, when she gives her memory, she gives everything that has happened. It is the inadequate religious woman who gives up *almost* everything in her past. But she is giving up "almost" everything. Her surrender is total with the exception of perhaps only one sin which she finds so unpardonable that she cannot give it up. She says she has confessed it. She says also she just cannot forgive herself for it. As long as she continues to cling to the guilt of this sin, she points an accusing finger at herself and says that she maintains a low evaluation of herself. Keeping herself thus in "the doghouse" she excuses herself from any sustained effort to be the real woman she might otherwise be.

Fr. Christoph: We torture ourselves by clinging to some memories we ought to forget. We cultivate scruples. Sometimes we get to the point where we think that we have committed the unforgivable sin. If we have given God everything, he accepts it, including the past as it is. This thought should be extremely relieving and satisfying to the individual.

There are things likewise to be remembered and cherished, especially those moments of consolation, those satisfying experiences that have brought us closer to God, whether through the agency of his creatures or by direct experiences. We treasure these consolations, but we are willing to surrender even them to God if he should choose to take them. We should not be upset because some of these satisfying spiritual experiences escape our memory. So if God blots them out of our memory, by our *suscipe* we accept it.

"And my understanding." Much earlier we raised the issue that even our Blessed Lady asked, "why?" "Why hast thou done so to us?" "How can this be?" We mentioned that this "why" is not the complaint of someone who is dissatisfied, but the "why" of ignorance. We offer him our understanding. Do we have to understand everything? First of all, we cannot. We know a good deal more in the natural order than we understand, and this is even more true in the supernatural order. Did we have a right to understand everything in our lives, we would be saying that we have a right to God's knowledge. No, we give him our understanding. Do you know what that means? We say in effect we will use it as he sees fit. If he wishes to give us more understanding, that is his to give or if he wishes to give us less, that is his to decide.

Fr. Evoy: This surrender of your understanding touches on something that is part and parcel of your being, your fascinatingly spontaneous curiosity. As a little child, you gave evidence of this curiosity in your oft repeated question, "why?" That early you were pointing out the truth that man, at his best, wants to know "why" about everything. Moreover, it seems to be according to man's nature that once he is satisfied that he does understand the reason for something, he can accept that thing as true.

Now in offering your understanding, you are openly telling God you will accept what he says, even though you may not grasp the "why" of it. In offering him your understanding you are doing something more than just accepting his revealed truth without demanding an explanation. In addition, you are dedicating your understanding to his service. This is saying that you will continue eagerly to ask "why" of so many things, in order better to be, for God, that which God wants you first of all to be—a

real woman. In addition, you will endeavor to employ the knowledge thus gained in ways you judge most pleasing to God. Hence
giving him your understanding means that you will lay down no
terms for accepting as true whatever he clearly reveals. It means,
as well, that you will continue to strive to understand everything
appropriate to your present position for his sake. You hope that
the understanding thus derived will ultimately be of some benefit
to other persons.

Fr. Christoph: St. Ignatius continues, "Dispose of them according
to thy good pleasure." St. Ignatius, in his prayer, is offering to
God everything. You should do likewise. You should offer to
Almighty God everything that you have in order to make yourselves the most suitable, the most intelligent real women in his
divine service.

An indication of our stewardship is expressed by St. Ignatius
when he says, "All that I am, and all that I have, thou hast given
me." We live in this world as in God's house. The things in it
are for us, but they are not ours. We are the guardians of these
things. We use them not any old way, but in the manner we
think and feel that God wants us to use them. This is the role
proper to the one who is a steward. Since we know that we must
exercise our stewardship reasonably and intelligently, we do it in
a more excellent way. We acknowledge that God has given us
these things, and we know he would be satisfied as long as we
would not abuse them. But we are religious and we give more
than the minimum; thus each of us says, "All that I am and have,
I give back to thee to be disposed of according to thy good
pleasure." "Not my will but thine be done" is all that is being
said here. Is all? That is everything, is it not?

The author of the Spiritual Exercises is aware that God is not
one who only receives. Above all, he is one who gives. So St.
Ignatius prays: "Give me only thy love and grace; with these I
am rich enough and ask no more." In saying this he seems to

recall Sacred Scripture: "Ask the Father anything in my name and it shall be given to you . . . Ask and you shall receive; seek and you shall find; knock and it shall be opened to you." Mindful that Christ himself said that he wants to be importuned, St. Ignatius then formulates his request, "Give me only thy love and grace."

We must not be deceived by the word "only." With God's love and grace we are in a position to be what God wants us to be. We are made for God, we are made to love God. Without the love of God our lives are barren. Possessing his love and grace, we are not only pleasing to him but also to our neighbor. "He who says he loves God and hates his neighbor, the truth is not in him and he is a liar." So when we ask with Ignatius for this love of God, we are implicitly saying, "God, help us to love our neighbor so we may deserve your love."

Fr. Evoy: Sisters, love God; love him completely with the love of a real woman. Love Christ in his Incarnate Person and in his Mystical Person with the personal love which is uniquely yours.

Fr. Christoph: Do not try to love him as does Mother Foundress, Sister Polycarp, or anyone else. Just love him the best way *you* know how, but love him as *you* are—a real woman.

Fr. Evoy: Be the best *you* for him. This is your ultimate aim. In this final encounter with Christ, we confront a very strong man, a very courageous man, but also a very gentle man. Note that the term "gentleman" is composed of the two words "gentle" and "man." Our Lord during his visible life on earth was a *real* man inspiring fear in those who attacked his own. But he was a *gentle* man. The little children did not hesitate to come to him. The people who were really hurting sought him. He was gentle; he was kind; he was meek, not weak. He *really* cared. The woman with the flow of blood, he healed. The bent reed, he did not break.

I think you could spend the rest of the year simply looking at the personality of Christ as he shows himself to you in the Scriptures. You encounter Christ therein as a dreamer of dreams. He has a cause such as no one has ever dared to dream of before. He would rule not only the entire world but over the heart and soul of every man, woman, and child. No one else has ever dared that.

It follows therefore that honestly and fully throwing in your lot with Christ, you cannot lose because he cannot lose and he loves you. Moreover, he will never ask you to do anything that he has not done ahead of you. He is your leader. Your generous living of your vows he accepts as the unquestionable evidence of your personal love for him.

In your tabernacle, the triumphant, gloriously risen, magnificent Christ, looking at each one of you, lovingly asks, "Will you continue to follow me as you have vowed to do—as a real woman?"

Suggested Books for Meditative Reading

Abbott, S.J., Walter, ed., *The Documents of Vatican II*. New York: America Press, 1966.

Cooke, S.J., Bernard, *Christian Involvement*. Chicago: Argus, 1966.

————, *Christian Sacraments and Christian Personality*. New York: Rinehart & Winston, 1965.

De Chardin, S.J., Teilhard, *The Divine Milieu*. New York: Harper, 1960.

Dondero, Brother Austin, *No Borrowed Light*. Milwaukee: Bruce, 1965.

Evely, Louis, *Suffering*. New York: Herder & Herder, 1967.

————, *That Man is You*. Westminster, Maryland: Newman Press, 1964.

Greeley, Andrew, *The Hesitant Pilgrim*. New York: Sheed & Ward, 1966.

Haring, C.Ss.R., Bernard, *Christian Maturity*. New York: Herder & Herder, 1967.

O'Keefe, S.S.N.D., Sister Maureen, *Christian Love in Religious Life*. Chicago: Regnery, 1965.

Rahner, S.J., Karl, *Christian Commitment*. New York: Sheed & Ward, 1963.

Thorman, Donald, *The Christian Vision*. New York: Doubleday, 1967.